Surviving Your Child's Adolescence Endorsements

Buddy Mendez has made an incredible impact, in our church and community. I highly recommend anything he writes including, *Surviving Your Child's Adolescence.*

—Eric Geiger, Senior Pastor, Mariners Church

⌒─✦─⌒

"Parents of teens are often confused about both navigating the long-term direction of their kid, as well as anxious about solving the near-term struggles that come up so frequently. They need healthy balanced perspective for the first, and practical tools to deal with the second. Buddy Mendez's book is a great contribution at both levels, bringing sanity, happiness and direction to their relationships with their adolescents. Highly recommended."

—John Townsend, Ph.D.
New York Bestselling author of the Boundaries series
Founder, Townsend Institute for Leadership and
Counseling and Townsend Leadership Program

⌒─✦─⌒

Parenting a teenager can sometimes feel like you're navigating an important journey without a map. With this book, Dr. Mendez not only provides clear direction, he serves as a compassionate guide to helping you become the best parent you can be. How? By understanding the deep and abiding needs your child has — and showing you how to meet them. Don't miss out on this grounded and practical message.

—Les Parrott, Ph.D.
#1 New York Times bestselling author of *Saving Your Marriage Before It Starts* and *Helping your Struggling Teenager*

SURVIVING
YOUR CHILD'S
ADOLESCENCE

A Christian Guide for Meeting Your
Teen's Deepest Needs

BUDDY MENDEZ, Ph.D.

WESTBOW
PRESS®
A DIVISION OF THOMAS NELSON
& ZONDERVAN

WestBow Press books may be ordered through booksellers or by contacting:

WestBow Press
A Division of Thomas Nelson & Zondervan
1663 Liberty Drive
Bloomington, IN 47403
www.westbowpress.com
844-714-3454

ISBN: 978-1-6642-2024-9 (sc)
ISBN: 978-1-6642-2026-3 (hc)
ISBN: 978-1-6642-2025-6 (e)

Library of Congress Control Number: 2021901509

Print information available on the last page.

WestBow Press rev. date: 3/2/2021

To Aaron, Brennon, Malia, and Blake. Thank you for teaching me so much about parenting. Your feedback, grace, and support have blessed me more than you can ever imagine.

Contents

Introduction

"Adolescents are walking contradictions." I often quote this phrase to my clients, colleagues, friends, and even family members. It seems that teenage behavior is often confusing and at times even paradoxical. No wonder parenting adolescents is so challenging. Adolescents beg for independence yet depend on parents to feed them, clothe them, and clean up after them. Adolescents prefer solving problems alone and yet often ask parents to rescue them from trouble. They want parents to be interested and attentive, yet they complain about parents being intrusive and smothering. My twenty-nine-year-old once said during his teenage years that we were like a dark shadow that followed him wherever he went. Adolescents cringe when parents hug them, yet they nestle into Mom's arms in times of distress. Adolescents threaten to move away as soon as possible, yet they are anxious about moving out. Parenting an adolescent can seem confusing at best and exhausting at worst. The truth is that adolescents need both independence and dependence, both autonomy and connection, and both our interest and our disinterest. Although teens may try to look like adults, they still have several psychological needs that parents are uniquely positioned to meet.

It is normal for parents to feel unprepared for the daunting task of navigating through the adolescent years. Because of the trepidation often associated with this important challenge, I chose to write this book. My aim is to help parents help their teenagers. This book is an antidote to what I so often witness in my work as a clinical psychologist. I have seen hundreds of adolescents who exhibit a wide variety of presenting problems and symptoms, which are actually disguised manifestations of unmet psychological needs. Wise parents focus on the satisfaction of these underlying psychological needs. In this book, I have chosen to explore ten primary developmental needs from both psychological and biblical perspectives. I have applied my personal experience as a parent of four teenagers, a full-time university professor, and a clinical psychologist in private practice. I hope and pray this book will better equip parents to meet the deepest needs of their sometimes perplexing and always cherished sons and daughters.

1

DISCERNMENT

Do not be conformed to this world, but be
transformed by the renewal of your mind, that by
testing you may discern what is the will of God,
what is good and acceptable and perfect.
—Romans 12:1–2

Walk as children of light (for the fruit of light is
found in all that is good and right and true), and try
to discern what is pleasing to the Lord.
—Ephesians 5:8–10

GOD HAS GIVEN parents the mandate to "train up a child in
the way he should go" (Proverbs 22:6). What does this mean? First,
parents use everything they know about their son or daughter to
discern the purposes God has uniquely designed them to pursue.
Second, parents do everything possible to create an environment
where the fulfillment of their purpose is most likely to occur. There
are two important areas where parental discernment is vital to the
health and well-being of adolescents. The first is what I call divine
design. The second I simply call character.

Divine Design

Divine design refers to the biblical truth that every person has a unique plan and means for glorifying God. The prophet Jeremiah writes, "For I know the plans I have for you, declares the Lord, plans for welfare and not for evil, to give you a future and a hope" (Jeremiah 29:11). It is vital that parents make every effort to discern the unique design of their teenager so they can best facilitate the fulfillment of God's plan for his or her life. In my private practice, one of the most common mistakes I see is that parents think it is their responsibility to *determine* how their teenager should live in order to find meaning, purpose, and ultimately fulfillment in life. Instead, the Bible teaches that parents should *discern* the "way" God has uniquely designed their son or daughter. Paul confirms this in his letter to the Ephesians: "For we are God's workmanship, created in Christ Jesus for good works, which God prepared beforehand that we should walk in them" (Ephesians 2:10).

Charles Swindoll (1988) has fully articulated this perspective in his book *Growing Wise in Family Life*. Swindoll offers a very helpful understanding of the parenting advice given in the book of Proverbs: "Train up a child in the *way* he should go; even when he is old he will not depart from it" (Proverbs 22:6). Swindoll believes that the Hebrew word for "way" refers to the unique manner in which God has created children. He further notes that the same Hebrew word translated as "way" (i.e., "darkov") also occurs in Proverbs 30:18–19, which says:

> Three things are too wonderful for me, four I do not understand: the *way* of an eagle in the sky, the *way* of a serpent on a rock, the *way* of a ship on the high seas, and the *way* of a man with a virgin. (emphasis added)

In this passage, the "way" of a child is not only beautiful but also beyond human understanding. Thus, the divine purpose for all of God's children is to become the person who God has intended for them to be. God alone *determines* the right path for an adolescent. It is the task of parents to *discern* this path. I often share the following metaphor with my clients to illustrate this point.

Teenagers are like different types of fruit trees—some apple trees, some orange trees, some peach trees, and some pear trees. The purpose of an apple tree is to produce apples, not oranges. The purpose of a peach tree is to produce peaches and not pears. A good farmer can discern what type of tree is growing in his or her field even before the tree bears fruit. Once the farmer discerns what tree he or she is cultivating, it is easier to decide what the optimal amount of water, sunlight, and nutrients are necessary to produce the best possible fruit for that particular tree.

Proverbs 22:6 instructs parents to be like the farmer. First, parents need to discern what type of "tree" God has given them. Second, parents must develop an individualized approach to parenting based on what method of care will yield the best fruit. If parents treat an apple tree like a peach tree, the apple tree may not produce any fruit.

I remember my son Brennon developing a unique passion for cooking at a very young age. While other teens were playing video games and competing in sports, Brennon preferred hanging out in the kitchen preparing various dishes from a variety of cultures. Believing that his interest and ability to cook was part of his very makeup as a child of God, I nurtured his natural interest in cooking by taking him to fine dining restaurants, arranging meetings with top restaurateurs in Southern California, and visiting chefs in other locales during family vacations. In fact, I even I bought him a textbook from the Culinary Institute of America for his tenth birthday. (He read it cover to cover in less than a week.) My mother even pitched in by hiring experienced chefs to provide private cooking lessons at her home. She graciously gave Brennon an open invitation to experiment in her kitchen (she also volunteered to pay for the ingredients and to clean up after him as long as she could enjoy what he prepared).

Brennon's ability and interest in cooking accelerated at a rapid pace. Today, at the age of twenty-five, he still loves cooking. Although he has decided to attend law school rather than become a chef, he is still able to glorify God by providing delicious meals during holidays and special occasions to the delight of his family and friends.

There are many ways to discern an adolescent's calling in life. First, we need to pay attention to the gifts, abilities, interests, and passions we observe in our sons and daughters. Knowing these things is the first step. Second, we need to make every effort to provide opportunities and nurturing environments that facilitate the development of the gifts, abilities, interests, and passions we observe. In chapter 10, I will elaborate on ways parents can create a positive environment that empowers adolescents to live a life in alignment with God's plans and purposes.

Character

The second important area for parents to discern is character. From my perspective, character reflects both the personality traits and inclinations of an adolescent. Knowing an adolescent's character allows parents to work smarter rather than just harder. Although every teenager is unique, it is possible to identify particular character traits that different groups of adolescents often share in common. Parrott and Parrott (2009) have written about four such clusters of traits in their book *L.O.V.E.: Putting Your Love Styles to Work for You*. In this book, the authors refer to four primary love styles, which I see as analogous to character styles. Although the authors discuss the love styles across all ages, I am going to limit my discussion to adolescents. My experience as a parent, professor, and psychologist is that adolescents can usually relate to one or two of the love styles. The authors make it easy to remember the four styles since the first letter of each love style spells out the word *love* (leaders, optimists, validators, and evaluators). Below, I describe my own understanding of each love style and make recommendations as to how parents can love their sons and daughters in specific ways.

Leaders

Leaders are direct and to the point in their communication, and they want their parents to be the same way. They will tune out if parents are too wordy. Leaders have difficulty attending to conversations they find disinteresting. They are quick to share their ideas, solutions, and advice, but they do not like taking the advice of others. Leaders usually believe they are right, and they can easily become argumentative and defiant if parents try to convince them otherwise. They prefer independence, power, and control in their lives. Leaders are willing to take on the workload and responsibilities that come with being a leader because the perceived benefits of being in charge outweigh the costs of the extra stress and work.

A great way to love a leader is to give him or her short and clear answers. It is important with leaders to hold your ground in order to maintain your authority. If you do not stand firm, the leader will quickly lose respect for you and take advantage of your perceived weakness by pushing boundaries and limits. It is helpful to give leaders plenty of opportunities to be in charge. In addition, leaders enjoy new and varied activities. They will often have new and creative ideas for how things can be better. It is important to consider their ideas and to give them credit when these ideas lead to positive results.

Leaders typically learn by doing. They tend to move fast without fully considering the consequences of their actions. They need parents to walk the balance between encouraging them to try new things while also slowing them down when their haste could lead to harmful consequences. It may sometimes be necessary to make leaders finish what they start, but it is not helpful to curb their desire to explore, seek out adventure, and try out new things.

Optimists

Optimists are emotional and enthusiastic communicators. They seeks out animated reactions from others, especially if they are excited about something. Optimists love to entertain others, and they never let the facts get in the way of a good story. They may take a while to get to the point, and their words should not be interpreted literally, especially when they are trying to express feelings. Optimists can be very sensitive to tone of voice and facial expressions. They love encouraging others and being encouraged by others. Optimists love people and especially love being around energetic, positive, and fun-loving people. They are usually concerned about how they look to others and will often adjust their behavior accordingly.

Optimists need parents who will listen with genuine enthusiasm to their ideas and stories and who will give animated and positive feedback frequently. They need plenty of time for fun social activities, especially with friends and family. Optimists sometimes will overcommit and wear themselves out. This means they need to rest and cut back if they overcommit to social activities. Optimists frequently seek out the admiration of their peers and parents. They enjoy entertaining others and having a good laugh. Optimists need parents to support their friendships and to understand their need to prioritize relationships over tasks. It is important to give optimists plenty of outlets for creative expression and to limit tasks involving attention to detail. Optimists love to feel important for being dynamic, vibrant, and fun loving. They usually feel better after they have vented their feelings without feeling judged or condemned.

Validators

Validators need time to process their thoughts and feelings internally before they speak. They are natural listeners who offer understanding and support without judgment. Validators prefer to speak through actions rather than words. They can be slow to share their own ideas, opinions, and feedback, especially if it is critical. Conflict makes validators anxious, and therefore they tend to avoid conflict like the plague. They prefer to yield to the wishes of others even when they have a different preference or perspective. Validators love peace and harmony in relationships and are careful to not say or do things that may upset others.

Validators need security, stability, and a calm presence in the home. They love it when the day goes according to plan with no surprises or conflicts. They enjoy sincere appreciation privately but often get uncomfortable being recognized in public settings. Validators prefer to stay under the radar and behind the scenes when they help others. They love people and are very loyal and trustworthy friends. Validators can easily be hurt because of their sensitivity. Therefore, it is helpful to periodically check in with them and ask them what they are thinking since they typically will not self-disclose without prompting. Validators need ample time to make decisions. When it comes to everyday tasks, they prefer to know in detail how others want things done. Although they are not big talkers and may have a limited friend group, validators cherish their friends and family and often spend lots of time and energy maintaining and nourishing these relationships.

Evaluators

Evaluators often ask *why* questions. They listen carefully to assess rather than to support. Evaluators tend to discredit those who are inaccurate. They value precision and quality. Evaluators love quality time and look for ways to be more efficient and effective with their time. They are systematic and organized in their thoughts and conversations.

Evaluators need quiet time to recharge. They crave recognition for their work ethic and their commitment to high standards of excellence. Evaluators enjoy it when others show respect for their knowledge and expertise. They prefer questions about their thoughts as opposed to their feelings. Evaluators love to plan and organize, and they may get anxious when a clear plan is not in place or the outcome is uncertain due to forces beyond their control. Evaluators become anxious when there is too much ambiguity or chaos in their environment. They prefer an orderly and streamlined life. Evaluators have little patience for the frivolous, unimportant, and the irrelevant. They avoid conversations with persons they perceive as uninformed. Evaluators value task accomplishment over relational sensitivity.

Concluding Thoughts

I recently received a heartwarming birthday card from my seventeen-year-old son Blake. I was amazed at how the words he wrote so clearly reflected his desire to become all that God has created him to be. I was also pleased to see that he recognizes my efforts to facilitate his maturing into his God-given design.

> Happy Birthday Dad. It is hard to put into words how much you mean to me but I will try my best. Over the past few years, I have seen your love and your dedication to make me the best version of myself. Only recently, I have realized that I need to start doing my end and following through with the opportunities, you have given me. My goal is to make you proud that you raised a son who doesn't stop working until he gets what he wants, but glorifies God while doing it.

DISCIPLINE

For the Lord disciplines the one he loves, and he chastises every son whom he receives. It is for discipline that you have to endure. God is treating you as sons. For what son is there whom his father does not discipline? If you are left without discipline, in which all have participated, then you are illegitimate children and not sons. Besides this, we have had earthly fathers who disciplined us and we respected them. Shall we not much more be subject to the Father of spirits and live? For they disciplined us for a short time as it seemed best to them, but he disciplines us for our good, that we may share his holiness. For the moment all discipline seems painful rather than pleasant, but later it yields the peaceful fruit of righteousness to those who have been trained by it.
—Hebrews 12:6–11

ALTHOUGH MOST ADOLESCENTS refuse to admit it, they genuinely have a deep desire for parental structure and discipline.

In homes where discipline is fair and consistent, adolescents experience safety and security. The Bible has much to say about the nature and benefits of discipline. Below are three important themes from Hebrews 12:6–11.

1. *Discipline is not punishment.* Discipline means to teach or train children to behave in ways that honor and glorify God. The goal of discipline is to facilitate the growth and development of children. On the other hand, punitive reactions are shortsighted and emanate out of a parent's frustration and anger. Discipline is a means to an end. Punishment is an end in itself.

2. *Discipline is a necessary component of love.* Contrary to popular opinion, discipline is not opposed to love but rather an essential aspect of love. Hebrews 12:6 says, "The Lord disciplines the one he loves and chastises every son whom he receives." In addition, Proverbs 13:24 says, "Whoever spares the rod hates his son, but he who loves him is diligent to discipline him."

3. *Discipline seems painful at the time, but the result is progress toward righteousness.* Discipline often results in pain. However, pain does not necessarily equal harm. In fact, effective discipline leads to righteousness (Hebrews 12:6), peace, and holiness of life (Hebrews 12:14). I remember being surprised to see how calm and respectful my children responded after I had disciplined them. When adolescents know that parents will keep them in bounds, they feel a sense of safety. This sense of safety soothes feelings of anxiety and tension. This is not to say that adolescents consciously welcome their parents' discipline. At a surface level, adolescents often seem averse to discipline. However, when parents maintain discipline without regard to protests, adolescents become more relaxed, respectful, and enjoyable to be around.

In my private practice, parents often express the desire to effectively discipline their adolescents but have no idea how to do it. Unfortunately, effective discipline is not instinctual. Rather, parents need to learn practical and proven methods of effective discipline from competent teachers. In my private practice, I help parents to be effective in their discipline by paying attention to three important things: clear rules, follow-through, and consistency.

Clear Rules

Parents must communicate what they expect from their teen. This means having clear and specific rules. These rules should include time element words whenever possible, such as *always* and *never*. Below is a sample list of rules for adolescents:

- Always complete your chores on time and without being asked.
- Always comply with parental requests immediately.
- Never argue, talk back, or interrupt anyone.
- Never hit, yell, or throw things at anyone or anything.
- Always be polite and kind by saying please and thank you.
- Always complete all homework before you engage in free time activity.
- Always abide by your driving contract. (This assumes you have a written, detailed, and specific driving contract signed by your adolescent.)
- Always be home on weeknights by ten o'clock and on weekends by midnight.
- Only buy and wear clothes that have been deemed appropriate by Mom and Dad.
- Always tell the truth.

Follow-Through

Follow-through refers to how parents respond in order to ensure adolescents comply with the family rules. It is important to note here that it is normal for adolescents to break rules. This typically happens for two reasons. First, because of their human fallibility. The Bible teaches, "For all have sinned and fall short of the glory of God" (Romans 3:23). Second, adolescents often unconsciously test to see if parents will have the courage and stamina to follow through on the rules in the midst of what I call "negative noise." (i.e., adolescents whining and complaining about rules and consequences in order to wear the parent down so the parent will back down and change his or her mind).

When adolescents fail to comply with rules, it is important for parents to not view the defiance as an attempt to frustrate them or as an indication that the adolescent is ungrateful and entitled. Rather, noncompliance often is simply an adolescent's unconscious bid for reassurance. Adolescents need to know that we will keep them safe and protect them from their own impulses. This way of thinking represents an important paradigm shift and makes it much easier to resist the impulse to shame or belittle adolescents.

Below are four useful follow-through techniques:

Reinforce the Positive

The first and most powerful follow-through technique is to reinforce adolescents when they comply with the rules. The best method of reinforcement is a word of affirmation given in a casual manner. For example, if your adolescent does his or her chores without prompting and on time, you can respond by saying, "Hey, Blake. Thanks for taking out the trash barrels last night. I love your idea of taking them out last night so you don't have to worry about doing it this morning." In addition, you can praise your adolescent when he or she acts in ways that are opposite of prohibited behavior. For instance, if you have a rule that says, "Never yell at your brother," you can say, "Thanks, Malia, for speaking calmly with your brother when he was annoying you." The idea here is that adolescents will be more likely to increase behavior that we reward rather than decrease behavior we punish.

Natural Consequences

The second effective follow-through technique is natural consequences. The idea with natural consequences is to stay out of the way of the consequences that follow an adolescent's poor choices. For example, if your teenager gets a ticket for speeding, the natural consequence is that he or she will have to pay a fine. If you pay the fine, then you are getting in the way of the natural consequence. It is better to make the adolescent pay for the ticket. Many parents get in the way of natural consequences because of what I call "subjective guilt." Subjective guilt is the guilt we feel when our adolescents express pain because of a poor decision on their part. When adolescents fully experience the natural consequences of their actions, they learn and grow from the experience. Giving into our own subjective guilt and rescuing our adolescents from their natural consequences will not help them mature.

Logical Consequences

The third effective follow-through technique is logical consequences. This refers to a consequence imposed by a parent after becoming aware of a rule violation. Good, logical consequences are creative and powerful enough to curb misbehavior. In addition, a good logical consequence has what I call the three Ss: simple, soon, and salient.

Simple

Logical consequences are more likely to occur in a consistent manner if they are not too complicated. For example, if a teenager refuses to eat dinner, a complicated consequence would be to prohibit the adolescent from eating food for the rest of the evening. It is complex because, in order to follow through, a parent has to watch the adolescent like a hawk the entire evening. A better consequence would be to take away the privilege of taking the adolescent out for frozen yogurt after dinner. This is much easier to follow through on. If he or she refuses to eat dinner, then you simply refuse to take him or her out for frozen yogurt.

Soon

Logical consequences work best when they occur as soon as possible. For example, if your teenager refuses to clean his or her room when asked, an appropriate consequence would be to take away the privilege of using all devices, such as the phone, computer and television, until he or she has cleaned the room. This is better than taking away the privilege of going out on the weekend. The weekend may still be days away, and the adolescent may be less inclined to clean his or her room in a timely manner.

Salient

Finally, effective logical consequences are salient. Salient means that the consequence has teeth in it. It has the power to prevent the reoccurrence of misbehavior in the future. For example, if your daughter is dressed inappropriately for a party, you can immediately donate whatever she is wearing to charity. You know this will be salient because adolescents typically are not going to wear clothing they do not like, and they do not want to do anything to lose clothing they love. Another example is an adolescent boy who fails to clean his bathroom. A salient consequence would be to require him to clean his bathroom and to clean every other bathroom in the house.

An important principle to follow when implementing a salient consequence is to use the minimum necessary strength. If we use a stronger consequence than is necessary to achieve the targeted positive behavior, we run the risk of unnecessarily exasperating our adolescent. This hinders our relational connection. Remember what Paul said in Colossians 3:21, "Fathers, do not provoke your children, lest they become discouraged."

The When/Then Principle

The when/then principle is a simple yet powerful discipline technique. It is especially useful to motivate adolescents to do things they do not want to do. To implement this method, say the following: "When you do X (something they don't want to do), then you can do Y (something they want to do)." For example, if your teenager wants desperately for you to drive him or her to the beach to meet up with friends, you can say, "Sure. I will take you as soon as you clean your room and finish your homework." Not only will your adolescent be motivated to complete these unpleasant tasks, he or she will most likely complete these tasks quickly, because the quicker he or she finishes, the sooner he or she will get to the beach. A note of advice here is that it is important to check that your adolescent has completed the necessary tasks according to your standards (not his or hers).

Consistency

Rules need to be consistent. Some modifications are fine, but once you establish a rule, stick with it. For example, you may want to stick with the same bedtime on a nightly basis, but be open to modifying the bedtime for weekends, summer, and as your adolescent ages. In addition, it is helpful to present house rules to your adolescent in written form so he or she will be less likely to feign ignorance regarding the existence of a particular rule.

Consistency needs to apply to the method, intensity, and duration of the follow-through technique. For instance, if the consequence for forgetting morning chores is thirty minutes of extra chores immediately after your adolescent gets home from school, it is best to stick with that precise consequence every time the morning chores are not completed. Do not change the nature of the consequence to something else, such as not being able to go to a friend's house that evening. Stay consistent with the consequence of extra chore time. Also, do not change the intensity to fifteen minutes of extra chore time because your adolescent looks tired or up it to forty-five minutes or thirty minutes for the rest of the week because you don't like his or her attitude.

As we attempt to apply consistent follow-through techniques, it is normal for adolescents to test our resolve. For example, they may try to persuade us to let them do a consequence after they complete their homework because they are stressed, or after they have a snack because they are starving, or after they counsel their best friend who is in crisis. Do not be swayed by these maneuvers. These are all typical examples of unconscious attempts to test our resolve. If we hold our ground, despite their protests, we will notice a gradual decrease in these types of unconscious tests over time. On the other hand, if we fail these tests, we can expect more frequent testing in the future.

Finally, it is crucial that both parents maintain a united front with regard to the establishment and enforcement of the rules. If only one parent follows through, a higher incidence of rule breaking will occur. If parents disagree on a rule or consequence, it is best to abide by the wishes of the more permissive parent.

Final Tips

In addition to clear rules, follow-through, and consistency, I recommend the following practical tips for effective discipline:

Be Gentle with Your Speech

Proverbs 15:1 states, "A soft answer turns way wrath, but a harsh word stirs up anger." I advise parents to speak slowly and softly as they consistently follow through on imposing consequences for misbehavior. This preserves the relational connection and keeps adolescents calm while maintaining a safe and secure environment.

Avoid Shaming and Belittling

Proverbs 12:18 says, "There is one whose rash words are like sword thrusts, but the tongue of the wise brings healing." We need to think before speaking, lest we run the risk of discouraging our adolescent. Paul warns against this danger in Colossians 3:21: "Fathers, do not provoke your children, lest they become discouraged." A common form of shaming involves asking why questions such as these:

> "Why didn't you call me?"
> "Why can't you do your chores when I ask you?"
> "Why don't you tell me the truth?"
> "Why don't you think before you act?"
> "Why don't you listen?"
> "Why don't you think about my feelings?"
> "Why do you have to be so stubborn?"
> "Why can't you think of anyone other than yourself?"

In the short run, shaming and belittling may seem to work. However, over time, shaming deeply hurts adolescents. A discouraged adolescent is more likely to turn feelings of shame inward by becoming more depressed and anxious or by acting out his or her shameful feelings by behaving in shameful ways.

Avoid Arguments

In 1 Timothy 3:3, Paul encourages believers to avoid quarrels. The easiest way for parents to follow this advice is to never waver when saying yes or no. Jesus captures the spirit of this principle when he exhorts his disciples to "Let what you say be simply Yes or No; anything more than this comes from evil" (Matthew 5:37). For example, if I tell my son Blake I will take him dirt bike riding on an upcoming weekend, and I then change my mind at the last minute, I have undermined my relational integrity and most likely decreased my son's trust and goodwill toward me. Therefore, it is vital that when parents say yes, they make every effort to be faithful to that promise.

On the other hand, it can be damaging to our authority and peace in the home when we change a no answer to a yes answer. For example, if my son Blake asks me if he can spend the night at a friend's house, even though he has a hockey game early the next morning, I most likely will respond with a resounding no, citing the fact that he will likely stay up too late and be exhausted for his game. If Blake really wants to spend the night at his friend's house, he may argue with me. He may try to persuade me to reconsider my decision by relentlessly arguing his case. As I have said earlier, I call this phenomenon making negative noise. Negative noise can take the form of whining, complaining, or arguing until the parent cannot take it anymore and caves in and changes the no to a yes. In my example with Blake, it is crucial that I hold to my no for one minute longer than Blake tries to get a yes. Even though a switch to yes will eliminate the negative noise in the short run, it will only exacerbate the use of the negative noise technique in the future. This creates a more argumentative teenager, a resentful parent, and a less peaceful home.

A second way to reduce arguing is to employ what Gregory Bodenhamer has termed argument deflectors (nevertheless, regardless, whether or not) (Bodenhamer 1984), followed by the phrase "anything else," which eventually ends the argument. The following dialogue demonstrates the effective use of these words and phrases:

Blake: "Hey, Dad, can I spend the night at Max's house?"

Dad: "No, Blake. That would not be wise. You have a game tomorrow morning at seven o'clock. You need to be rested and ready to play."

Blake: "But, Dad, I promise we will go to bed early."

Dad: "Regardless of what time you promise to go to bed, my answer is no."

Blake: "But Max invited all of our friends. I don't want to miss out."

Dad: "Nevertheless, my answer is no."

Blake: "But you said you want me to have fun in high school and not always focus on academics and sports."

Dad: "Whether or not I said that, my answer is no."

Blake: "This isn't fair. You would let Malia go if she asked you."

Dad: "Is there anything else you want to say?"

Blake: "Can I go?"

Dad: "No. Is there anything else?"

Blake: "If I can't go, then I'm going to stay up late tonight anyways."

Dad: "Anything else?"

Blake: He says nothing else and goes to his room. (Note: If he stays up late, I will give him the consequence of early wake-up time for the rest of the week because this is easier to follow through on than an early bedtime.)

Optimal Frustration

As surprising as it may sound, it is not always a mistake to frustrate adolescents. When adolescents' wishes and requests are not immediately gratified, they are given the opportunity to exercise and develop the muscle that allows them to delay gratification and tolerate frustration. This muscle will come in handy when they inevitably face disappointment later in life. On the other hand, if adolescents are consistently and constantly frustrated in their efforts to get their needs met, they will become overly anxious and depressed. Balance is the key. We need to frustrate our adolescents just enough to build muscle but not so much that they become discouraged. The parents I work with in my private practice tend to error on the side of overgratification in terms of material possessions, privileges, and acts of service while at the same time undergratification in terms of empathy, emotional support, understanding, and the granting of personal autonomy and responsibility.

Modeling

The final discipline tip is to *be what you want to see*. Proverbs teaches this principle, "The righteous who walks in his integrity— blessed are his children after him!" (Proverbs 20:7). Adolescents often identify and emulate the lifestyle of their parents. Therefore, whatever you require of your teenager ought to be required of yourself. For example, preaching to your child abstinence from drugs and alcohol will not be effective if you are consistently drinking a bottle of wine every night with dinner. In the same way, yelling at your teenager to stop yelling at his or her younger brother or sister will not work. Finally, expecting your teenager to admit his or her mistakes and apologize for his or her hurtful actions is unrealistic and unfair if you as a parent are not willing to admit your mistakes and apologize when you have offended or hurt someone.

Case Study

To illustrate this model of discipline, I will use a real example from my teenage years. Shortly after turning sixteen and getting my driver's license, I did what many sixteen-year-olds do and got in my first car accident. I was backing out of my friend's driveway a little too fast while joking with him and neglecting to look behind me. As I turned to angle into the street, I smashed into the front end of his sister's Vega. She had parked it on the street next to the driveway. Unfortunately, I did not see her car until I had put a substantial dent in the front end.

I remember being terrified to face my parents when I came home. I was fighting off tears as I explained to them my mistake. I was afraid they would say I had been careless and irresponsible and was therefore not ready to drive. I expected my dad to hurl angry insults and my mom to ask me through tearful eyes where she had gone wrong as a mother.

Fortunately, that is not what happened. My parents were both calm and compassionate. They told me this was an unfortunate accident and that accidents happen to everyone. They reassured me that they forgave me and would help me to make things right with my friend's sister. They taught me about auto insurance claims, body shops, and deductibles. They advised me to accept responsibility by offering to pay for the necessary repairs. I remember withdrawing my life savings and doing extra work around the house to accumulate enough money to pay for the repairs. This experience turned out to be a valuable lesson for me and a great example of fair and effective discipline by my parents.

Sadly, many of the parents I counsel would not have handled this situation as well as my parents. Typically, I see parents who insult and belittle their teenager first and then proceed to pay for the cost of the mistake later. In addition, these parents revisit the mistake whenever they are upset with their teenager. When these parents revisit the incident, they never forget to restate how much money they had to pay in order to repair the damaged car. This process of shaming without imposing a logical consequence is completely backward, harming adolescents and stunting their growth and development.

CONNECTION

> Then the Lord God said, It is not good that the man should be alone.
>
> —Genesis 2:18a

> From whom the whole body, joined and held together by every joint with which it is equipped, when each part is working properly, makes the body grow so that it builds itself up in love.
>
> —Ephesians 4:16

GOD IS TRIUNE. His very nature is relational. We are created in His image (Genesis 1:27). As image bearers, we thrive when we live in harmonious relationships, just as God does as Father, Son, and Holy Spirit. The Bible puts it this way, "It is not good that the man should be alone" (Genesis 2:18a).

Many research studies have focused on the psychological benefits of human relational connection. Psychology researchers have discovered that children and adolescents thrive when they have responsive and reliable parent who provides a "secure base" to launch from and a "safe haven" to land (Bowlby 1988). Wilkinson

(2001) has found that for adolescents, the quality of the attachment to parents predicts increased well-being and decreased distress. More specifically, researchers have found a positive link between a strong attachment relationship and empathy, helping, and altruism (Panfile and Laible 2012). Finally, researchers have found that secure attachment predicts positive peer relations, healthy self-concept, and emotional regulation (Dykas, Ziv, and Cassidy 2008; Kobak and Sceery 1988).

How can parents form a healthy and secure attachment to their teenagers? Below I have listed ten practical ways to promote attachment based on my experience as an adolescent psychotherapist and a father of four adolescents.

Attunement

Adolescents need parents to tune in to what they are thinking, doing, and feeling. This process of aligning our own internal state with that of our teen is attunement. The best way to show attunement to is to listen well with genuine curiosity, concern, and interest in our teenager. It is well known that one of the most common complaints of adolescents is "My parents never listen." The book of Proverbs speaks to this common problem saying, "If one gives an answer before he hears, it is his folly and shame" (Proverbs 18:13).

I listen well when I think of myself as a biographical writer who needs to write an interesting story on the life experience of my teen. When I focus on myself as a writer, I ask good questions, listen to understand and not judge, and avoid common pitfalls like interrupting, lecturing, and giving quick advice. Thinking of myself as a writer also keeps me focused on my teen's experience rather than my own reaction to her experience. For example, if my daughter shares her dilemma over what prom dress to get, I need to resist the temptation of asking too quickly about prices if I worry that I may not be able to afford what she likes.

Parents who allow and tolerate silence have a greater chance of remaining attuned. Sometimes teenagers need time to process their thoughts and feelings. Silence allows them to do this. Lastly, it is helpful to remember what our teenagers have previously shared with us. This provides evidence that we are listening carefully. This is especially important when adolescents share the vulnerable parts of themselves or disclose private feelings.

Empathy

Heinz Kohut described empathy as the "capacity to think and feel oneself into the inner life of another" (Kohut 2013). Empathy allows teens to "feel felt." When parents empathize, we walk in the shoes of our teenager, doing our best to understand the world from his or her perspective. This means we seek to know what our teenager is thinking and feeling. More importantly, empathy allows parents to understand what meanings our adolescents ascribe to the world they live in through the lens of their own idiosyncratic experiences. Empathy is difficult. It takes effort, energy, patience, and practice. However, the benefits of empathy far outweigh the costs. When we prioritize and practice empathy, we convey a deep understanding of our teenager's state of mind and the fullness of his or her emotional experience. An easy way to know how to empathize is to *say what you see*. Empathic statements often start with an opening phrase such as one of these:

> It sounds like …
> It seems like …
> What I'm seeing is …
> What I'm hearing is …
> What I'm sensing is …
> I can see that …

For example, at the age of sixteen, my daughter, Malia, was invited to a prestigious conference at Facebook headquarters on the same weekend we had planned to visit colleges on the East Coast. Since our airfare and hotel reservations had already been booked, we sadly had to tell Malia that we could not reschedule the trip. She was extremely disappointed. This moment called for empathy because there was really nothing we could do to change the circumstances. This is what I said to Malia, to the best of my recollection: "Honey, I can see that you really wanted to go to the Inspire Ed conference this year, and you were really excited to be a VIP guest at Facebook headquarters. It must be so disappointing and frustrating that the dates for the conference fall on the same weekend we will be visiting colleges on the East Coast. It must be even more frustrating that we cannot change the dates of our college visits."

Involvement

Involvement means showing up for a teenager and taking an active interest in his or her life. Involved parents know what their adolescent's favorites are, whether it is food, music, friends, clothes, teachers, activities, art, poetry, books, sports, places, schools, or even favorite things he or she likes about them. Involvement means we are not just for our children, but we are also with them. We attend their big events and performances, and we celebrate their successes. We enjoy spending time with them. If we do not understand or know what they value, then we ask about it. In other words, if anything is important to them, it automatically becomes important to us.

It is especially important that parents attend adolescent events, activities, and performances, even if doing so may be inconvenient or feel awkward or uncomfortable. For example, my daughter's high school boyfriend, who ran cross-country for Orange Lutheran High School, had his parents travel to one of his races even though it was over an hour away from their home. The fact that they showed up was impressive in and of itself, but what really amazed me was that they both came with running shoes. This allowed them to run to five different locations throughout the fifteen-minute race in order to see their son as much as possible. Their commitment to involvement surprised and impressed me. In this particular case, their support may have even helped him run faster, since he cut his previous best time by over thirty seconds.

Another example of involvement comes from an adolescent client in my private practice. I remember one session asking her the question, "What experiences and memories do you have of feeling closely connected to your dad?" Her answer shocked me as she quickly responded, "This may sound crazy, but my father always drove me to my monthly orthodontist appointments, and I always felt close to him during those drives." Her example taught me that an act of involvement does not have to be flashy or fancy but rather just heartfelt and genuine.

Reassurance

A classic trait of teenagers is insecurity. Even if they will never admit it, teens are constantly looking for reassurance. I remember when my daughter received her first AP score her sophomore year of high school. She had taken AP Art History and prepared diligently for the AP test. As many of you may know, students can score between a one and a five on the AP test. Scores in the three to five range are passing. My daughter was hoping for a score of four or five. When she received her score of two, she fell apart on a level I have never seen before. There was crying and screaming, and there was lots of verbal self-denigration. She was inconsolable. I found it impossible to speak to her without upsetting her even more.

Finally, after about an hour of regrouping high on a sturdy branch of her favorite oak tree, she returned home in a better mental space. I was relieved that I let her go rather than trying to chase her down (I will discuss this more in chapter 6). When she returned, I could tell she had an unspoken need for connection and reassurance. I approached her and began to gratify these deep needs in large doses. I reminded her that one test score does not have the power to derail her future dreams. I also told her that there were many alternative explanations for her score and that I highly doubted she would ever score this low on an AP test again. I shared with her that God has a plan for her (Jeremiah 29:11) and one AP test score would not derail her from His plan. I reminded her that God causes all things to work together for His good (Romans 8:28). I hugged her and told her that even if she did not believe me, I knew that everything would work out and be OK. As I write, I can confidently say that things did work out very well for Malia. On subsequent AP tests, she scored either a four or a five. She finished Orange Lutheran High School with a 4.5 GPA, scored 34 out of 36 on her ACT test, and is now a junior at Stanford University.

Kindness

Kindness is the warm, authentic, and generous extension of care and compassion without expecting anything in return. The concept of not expecting anything in return is especially important when parenting teens. Teens are notorious for not expressing gratitude when parents are kind to them. This has to do with their developmentally appropriate self-preoccupation. Parents need to trust that acts of kindness benefit teenagers, even when teenagers seem ungrateful. The truth is that when parents are kind, adolescents subconsciously feel valued and supported.

For example, a few years ago, I gave my daughter a heartfelt birthday card with a generous cash gift tucked inside. I was somewhat surprised when she did not mention anything about it on her birthday. I confess that I even took a peak in her bedroom to see if she had opened it. To my surprise, it was open. I had to remind myself that the benefit of the gift was in no way diminished by the lack of her response. The next day, I received another surprise. My daughter thanked me for the gift and told me how excited she was to use the money for an upcoming service trip.

An act of kindness can communicate support and encouragement in a more powerful way than words. I remember when I was in the eighth grade and, despite the fact that my family lived on a shoestring budget, my dad bought me the most expensive basketball shoes on sale at the time: the Adidas Superstar. My dad understood not only my love for basketball but also my desire to be the best basketball player possible. I felt loved, but more importantly, I felt understood and grateful that my father chose to invest his best when it mattered most to his son.

Parents can express kindness in small and recurring acts of service. For example, my wife dedicated herself to preparing a nutritious and delicious breakfast and packed lunch for our teenage children every school day. She did this without any fanfare and with little overt gratitude. Like most parents, she often wondered if her efforts mattered to her children. I am sure when our teenagers start making meals for their own children, they will be sure to share their gratitude and how much these acts of kindness helped them to feel loved.

Respect

A strong connection thrives in an atmosphere of mutual respect. Parents expect children and adolescents to show proper respect. However, the Bible says that Christians should "Honor everyone" (1 Peter 2:17a). This means that we need to show proper respect to our children as well. Adolescents thrive when we treat them with dignity. Parents can do this is in simple ways, such as using please and thank you and asking for their help rather than demanding it. In addition, parents show respect when they do not try to convince their teens to think like them, dress like them, or adhere to their political views or cultural practices. Instead, parents should refrain from guilt trips or criticism, especially when their teens live in a manner that leaves parents feeling bewildered or even disappointed.

I remember when my daughter proclaimed to my wife and me that she was going to stop eating all meat except for fish. We were surprised but at the same time knew after hearing out her reasons that this was a decision she had thoughtfully considered. I remember telling her that although I personally could not imagine living a life without hamburgers and bacon, I fully supported her decision. On another occasion, I remember my oldest son, Aaron, telling me that he was going to work full-time instead of attending college. I also remember when Brennon told me he did not want to attend a private Christian high school. These were all tough choices for me to handle, but I knew they were important opportunities for me to respond with respect rather than criticism in order to maintain a strong relational connection.

Respect also increases when parents resist the urge to harbor resentment. Resentment is a normal feeling for parents to experience, especially when adolescents express criticism, sarcasm, and aggressive and passive-aggressive behavior. Resentment is corrosive to human connection. There are a plethora of unconscious reasons adolescents behave in ways that cause parents to feel resentment. First, adolescents can more comfortably practice autonomy when they see their parents as flawed and fallible. Seeing parents as imperfect makes it easier for adolescents to stop identifying with their parents in order to feel a solid and independent sense of self. The second reason adolescents behave in ways that lead to resentment is that they are unconsciously testing parents to see how well parents can handle criticism. When parents respond to criticism in a healthy way, they teach adolescents to more effectively deal with the increasing negativity the adolescent may experience with their peers and teachers and coaches.

How can parents manage feelings of resentment? I advise parents to see feelings of resentment as a possible signal that they need to make an immediate request. For example, a few years ago, my daughter told me in front of my wife and her best friend that I was grumpy and irritable. I was surprised to hear this since in my mind I had been making every effort to be kind and lighthearted. I knew my daughter and I were both a little extra sensitive since she was on the cusp of moving out to college. I felt hurt, embarrassed, and even resentful. I knew that I did not want to hold resentment toward her, so I asked myself two important questions: *First, how can I respond in a wise and respectful manner? Second, what would be a reasonable request?* I decided to text her so she would get an immediate request, without embarrassing her in front of her mother and best friend. In my text, I apologized for seeming grumpy and irritable. Next, I shared my hurt feelings. Then I made my request. I asked her to let me know as soon as possible when she experiences me negatively, rather than bring it up in front of family and friends. I went up to my room to brush my teeth (and decompress). Within a minute of sending this text, she was knocking at my bedroom door. She came to apologize. We talked for a few minutes, and then she asked if we were OK. I said yes, knowing that my feelings of resentment had completely evaporated from my heart and mind.

Understanding

Proverbs 16:22a says, "Good sense is a fountain of life to him who has it." A common lament I hear in my counseling office is "My parents just don't understand." Sometimes parents get so anxious about what they are hearing from their teen they immediately jump into an advice-giving, problem-solving, or disciplinary mode. This ruptures the relational tie and often results in their teen becoming combative or withdrawn. A beneficial alternative would be to use phrases such as "That makes sense to me," "I can understand how you can feel like that," and "I see your point."

Another common barrier to understanding is failing to attribute an equal level of importance to an issue, conflict, or dilemma that is troubling your teenager. Remember that the teenage brain develops first in the emotional areas and lastly in the areas of higher order reasoning. This means that adolescents often appear to be harder hit emotionally and often experience transient disappointments as permanent disasters. It is easier for a teen to fail to see the big picture or the fleeting nature of his or her negative feelings. Therefore, it is common for teens to see an imminent crisis when parents see a brief setback. It is very helpful for building connection during these times to respond to the situation from the perspective of your adolescent. This will lead to a greater sense of felt understanding and in turn a greater feeling of connection.

Accepting Influence

When parents accept influence, they strengthen the self-esteem of their teenager. This is extremely valuable at the adolescent stage of development and often leads to an increased desire for relational connection. One Sunday after church, my son Blake and I drove home together. As I approached the intersection, I stayed in the far right lane in order to make a right-hand turn at the intersection. Blake said, "Hey, Dad, you can get in the left lane and still make a right turn." This was a great idea since the left lane was much less crowded. I almost reflexively said, "I'm fine." However, I realized this was an opportunity to show my then fourteen-year-old son that I was willing to accept his influence. I changed lanes and thanked my son for his idea. He smiled almost imperceptibly (as teens often do), but I knew I had just strengthened our relational connection through this simple gesture. Humility promotes the acceptance of influence. Do not let sinful pride interfere with the opportunity to connect with your teen.

Confession

Confession means that parents admit mistakes, acknowledge shortcomings, and apologize when necessary. This is easier to do when parents recognize the biblical truth we are all sinners saved by grace through faith and not by works (Ephesians 2:9). In other words, God does not expect perfection but rather confession and repentance. The gospel of John reads, "If we claim to be without sin, we deceive ourselves and the truth is not in us. If we confess our sins, he is faithful and just to forgive us our sins and to cleanse us from all unrighteousness" (1 John 1:9). Paul reminds us of our sinful condition in Romans, "For all have sinned and fall short of the glory of God" (Romans 3:23). The prophet Isaiah puts it this way: "All our righteous deeds are like a polluted garment" (Isaiah 64:6).

Good parenting is not about never making mistakes but rather confessing mistakes with humility. Confession leads to greater connection because it has the power to heal the inevitable relational ruptures between parents and adolescents. Support for this principle is found in the book of James: "Therefore confess your sins to one another and pray for one another, that you may be healed" (James 5:16).

A few years ago, I found myself in dire need of confession. At home, my then fourteen-year-old son, Blake, was trying his best to fasten a new hockey grip on the end of his brand-new hockey stick. He was having little success, so he asked me for help. I agreed but quickly realized that I was also unable to make the new grip fit right, despite my best efforts. I remember feeling frustrated and angry. Unfortunately, I did not handle my feelings very well. I blamed Blake when it became clear that we had no chance of getting the grip on correctly. Blake tried to defend himself, but I continued my attack as my frustration and anger escalated. Eventually, Blake could not take it anymore, and he ran upstairs.

At this point, I knew I was clearly in the wrong. I had just provoked my son to anger and possibly shame when he had done nothing wrong. In the midst of my despair, God spoke to me. I remembered that what hurts children the most is not the mistake itself but rather the lack of a heartfelt apology. At that moment, I knew I had to confess to my son. With an unsteady voice and a heart full of remorse, I told Blake I had made a serious mistake and I was very sorry. I confessed to him that I was wrong to blame him and that it was only my mistake that caused his distress. I asked him to forgive me. I told him I would make every effort to treat him with respect in the future. Thankfully, my son forgave me as he always does, and we are now closer because of it.

Appreciation

We can show appreciation to our teen by words of affirmation, words of gratitude, and words that remind him or her of his or her strengths and accomplishments. Proverbs says, "Gracious words are like a honeycomb, sweetness to the soul and health to the body" (Proverbs 16:24). Parents spend too much time asking teens to appreciate all that they do for them. It is not that parents do not do a lot for their teenage children. However, teenagers are not developmentally ready to acknowledge the wonderful contributions and sacrifices parents make on a regular basis. Unfortunately, when parents do not receive the affirmation and gratitude they feel they deserve, they become stingy handing it out to their teens. Although this is an understandable response, it is not helpful for building relational connection.

My suggestion to parents is actually quite counterintuitive. Praise your adolescent liberally and often. Do it casually without much fanfare, lest they perceive you as inauthentic. Say thank you when they are kind and considerate toward you. As a result, you will likely see your teenager begin to move toward you like a bee flying toward honey.

4

COMFORT

Love one another with brotherly affection.
—Romans 12:10

Blessed be the God and Father of our Lord Jesus
Christ, the Father of mercies and God of all
comfort, who comforts us in all our affliction, so
that we may be able to comfort those who are in
any affliction with the comfort with which we
ourselves are comforted by God.
—2 Corinthians 1:3–4

ADOLESCENTS NEED COMFORT like plants need water.
Comfort nourishes, sustains, and promotes an adolescent's growth
and well-being. When parents provide comfort on a consistent basis,
adolescents develop the capacity to comfort themselves. In other
words, an interpersonal process gradually becomes an intrapersonal
process with several repetitions. The ability to self-soothe allows
adolescents to thrive in the midst of difficult circumstances.

Here is a list of some helpful ways to comfort adolescents, gleaned
from my experience as a clinical psychologist and from scripture.

Encouragement

The Bible says that "gracious words are like a honeycomb, sweetness to the soul and health to the body" (Proverbs 16:24). The writer of Hebrews adds, "And let us consider how to stir up one another to love and good works" (Hebrews 10:24–25). Parents encourage adolescents by showing confidence in their capabilities. Parents can also encourage adolescents by reminding them that they are made in God's image (Genesis 1:27) and created to do good works (Ephesians 2:10).

Paul gives a great example of encouragement in his letter to the Philippians, saying, "I thank my God in all my remembrance of you, always in every prayer of mine for you all making my prayer with joy, because of your partnership in the gospel from the first day until now. And I am sure of this, that he who began a good work in you will bring it to completion at the day of Jesus Christ" (Philippians 1:3–6).

I remember sending a text to my son Blake that exemplifies verbal encouragement. Below is what I wrote:

> Hey Bubba. I forgot to tell you last night that I really liked the ending to the story you wrote. The ideas of having General Zaroff jump in the water and the fight at the house with Rainsford and then having Rainsford sleeping soundly in the General's bed were awesome. I love your creativity and the sense of action and suspense you created. I'm so proud of you for pushing through to get past the distractions and to get that assignment done. That is perseverance at its best and those traits will serve you well in life. Love you. Dad.

Imagine if you sent a similar text. After the initial shock, your teenager would likely feel loved, encouraged, and maybe even comforted.

Provide Meaningful Touch

A second way of comforting teenagers is to provide physical affection. Research has found that parental affection is one of the most important predictors of health-related quality of life in adolescence (Jimenez-Iglesias 2015). In the Bible, the apostle Paul exhorts us to "love one another with brotherly affection" (Romans 12:10). Affection can take the form of a hug, gentle touch, fist pump, or even a high five. Parents need to study their adolescent to know which gestures of physical affection are most meaningful.

For instance, my daughter, Malia, typically does not like to be touched unless she initiates contact first. However, when she leans in for a hug, she wants me to respond in kind. On the other hand, my son Blake will accept affection anytime, so feel I comfortable putting my arm around his shoulders even when he does not expect it.

A great example of the power of touch is the parable of the prodigal son. In this story, the wayward son returns to his father after squandering his inheritance. The son is ashamed and afraid that his father will respond to his return home with judgment and condemnation. Instead, the father comforts his son, not with words but rather with physical affection. Luke writes, "But while he was still a long way off, his father saw him felt compassion, and ran and embraced him and kissed him" (Luke 15:20). When was the last time you ran to your teenager and embraced them with a warm hug and a kiss? Maybe you could try this as an experiment. Their response may pleasantly surprise you.

Play

Proverbs 15:13 says, "A glad heart makes a cheerful face." One of the easiest ways to make the heart of an adolescent happy is through play. From a psychological perspective, research has found a significant relationship between family leisure and overall family functioning (Freeman and Zabriskie 2003).

Leisure activities can include everyday examples of enjoyable interactions, such as family meals, video games, board games, card games, playing sports, singing and listening to music, and arts and crafts. Leisure activities can also include novel activities, such as family vacations, camping, fishing, plays and concerts, amusement parks, and church and community events.

The onset of adolescence does not mean playtime is over. Even though teenagers may initially seem indifferent to playing with their family, they actually desire it in their heart of hearts. Enjoying a recreational activity with your adolescent may start out slow but end up completely enjoyable and gratifying.

One of the activities my family enjoys is dirt bike riding. We also enjoy vacationing in Hawaii, body surfing together at the beach, and playing sports together such as basketball, volleyball, and roller hockey. When we play together, our sense of togetherness, connection, and closeness naturally follows. For teenagers, experiencing family as a safe haven to relax and decompress can drastically counter the effects of stress. The pressure of college applications, schoolwork, social relationships, sports, and extracurricular activities can be relieved when families spend enjoyable time together.

Play frees adolescents. It liberates them. It relaxes them. Most importantly, it bonds them to parents and siblings. Play is the glue that keeps families stuck together. Unfortunately, a variety of factors such as busy schedules, increased emphasis on academics, and increased participation in extracurricular activities designed to bolster college applications often interfere with playtime. Another more recent obstacle to family leisure time together is social media. Often times, adolescents express an outward preference for PlayStation, Instagram, YouTube, or Snapchat rather than family time together. Parents must fight against this trend even if it means forcing adolescents to take social media and video game time-outs.

In addition to building family connection, play provides comfort and soothing to adolescents. Unlike adults, who often feel comforted through a supportive conversation, adolescents feel comforted by simply playing. For example, if an adolescent says, "I can't think about school anymore," and goes outside to shoot baskets, a discerning parent could ask to join them. Playing a game of horse or one-on-one may be exactly what your adolescent needs.

Pray with Your Teen

Praying is a fourth way parents can comfort anxious adolescents. Paul writes in his letter to the Philippians, "Do not be anxious about anything, but in everything by prayer and supplication with thanksgiving, let your requests be made known to God. And the peace of God, which surpasses all understanding, will guard your hearts and your minds in Christ Jesus" (Philippians 4:6–7). This is especially helpful in situations where teenagers feel helpless and powerless. It is comforting for adolescents when they trust that God has a plan and a purpose for their life and believe God will work everything together for His good (Romans 8:28).

Create Positive Memories of Relational Connection

I once had a client who told me that she wanted to spend her savings on providing experiences for her children rather than material possessions. I thought this was a wise approach. In times of distress, it is comforting to an adolescent to reflect, reminisce, and remember happier times when life felt exhilarating and enjoyable. Usually, these memories consist of pleasurable experiences with others with whom the adolescent shares deep connections. It usually isn't the *what* of the activity that provides the most comfort upon reflection but rather the *who* of the activity and the feelings experienced with the *who* of that particular experience. Parents allow for this by creating these gratifying experiences in the here and now.

An example of a memorable experience that my daughter, Malia, often shares with her friends is Thursday breakfasts with Dad at Ruby's. This is a tradition I started when Malia was in elementary school. Every Thursday morning, we would go Ruby's before I dropped her off at school. We had our own table with a spectacular view of the nearby lake and a fantastic and friendly server, Mare, who we both believe is the nicest person in the world. We always ordered the same thing, so upon our arrival, Mare would simply say, "The usual?" and we would nod yes. My daughter would talk about whatever was on her mind with vulnerability, authenticity, and candor. Even silence was OK. We just enjoyed being together and knowing that if anything crazy, exciting, or even disappointing happened during the week, there was always an opportunity for discussion on Thursday morning. This has and probably will always be a comforting memory for not only my adolescent daughter but for myself as well. I strongly encourage you to create your own Ruby's experience with your teenager. It may look different, but as long as it is memorable, your teenager will love it.

Forgive Your Teen

The story of Joseph and his brothers demonstrates the comforting power of forgiveness. In Genesis 50:15–18, Joseph's brothers express their fear that Joseph will hate them for their evil acts toward him. Because of their fear, they sent a message to Joseph pleading for his forgiveness. Joseph wept at the idea that his brothers would even consider that he would not forgive them. Verse 21 shows his compassion, "Thus he *comforted* them and spoke kindly to them" (Genesis 50:21).

Although we do not think of our teenagers as evildoers, we can all recall times when they needed our forgiveness. At these times, we need to be Joseph and not only offer forgiveness but do so in a kind manner.

Barriers to Comforting

There are several mistakes parents commonly make when trying to comfort their adolescent. The first mistake is to try to cheer up an adolescent when they feel down. The Bible says, "Whoever sings songs to a heavy heart is like one who takes off a garment on a cold day, and like vinegar on soda" (Proverbs 25:20). Parents who fail to listen carefully to the depth of their teenager's pain will likely push their teenager back into his or her shell. This happens because the teenager infers that his or her feelings may be of little interest or possibly even overwhelming to his or her parents. If this happens consistently, your teenager will develop the fear that an authentic expression of painful feelings is dangerous and best avoided. Your adolescent will then repress his or her negative feelings, and consequently, feelings of resentment, loneliness, anxiety, and depression may emerge. I counsel parents to initially and patiently explore and validate the painful feelings of their adolescent before offering a solution. In other words, it is a good practice for parents to first validate feelings and second to solve problems or give advice.

The second mistake parents often make is giving unrealistic positive feedback. For instance, if your adolescent comes in last place in a sprint race at a track meet, it is not helpful to tell him or her that he or she is a fast runner and must have had an off day. When your teenager hears this, he or she knows you are not being honest, and he or she will have a harder time believing positive feedback from you in the future, even when it is genuine. In the above example, even though the adolescent is a slow sprinter, he or she may be an excellent distance runner. If that is the case, parents are wise to reserve their praise for distance races. Proverbs supports this view as it says, "A lying tongue hates its victims and a flattering mouth works ruin" (Proverbs 26:28).

The third mistake occurs when parents are reckless with their words when they are frustrated with their teenager. It is OK for a parent to express feelings of anger and frustration. It is not OK to hurl insults. The Bible says that "there is one whose rash words are like sword thrusts, but tongue of the wise brings healing" (Proverbs 12:18). In addition, Paul writes, "Let no corrupting talk come out of your mouths, but only such as is good for building up, as fits the occasion, that it may give grace to those who hear" (Ephesians 4:29).

To sum up, parents who value encouragement, affection, play, prayer, forgiveness, and the creation of positive memories help adolescents internalize the ability to comfort themselves and self-soothe during inevitable experiences of stress and strain throughout the adolescent years.

5

IDENTITY

Beloved, we are God's children now, and what we will be has not yet appeared; but we know that when he appears we shall be like him, because we shall see him as he is.

—1 John 3:2

IDENTITY REFERS TO a person's sense of self. The establishment of a meaningful and coherent identity is the central developmental task of adolescence. Adolescents achieve their identities as they examine their God-given feelings, attitudes, intentions, beliefs, and values and explore new and different ways of relating to their interpersonal world. Healthy adolescents gradually discover how they are similar and/or different from others through the process of exploration and eventually commitment. Research shows that a stable and strong sense of identity is positively associated with several measures of psychological adjustment and well-being (Rageliene 2016). In order to consolidate an identity, adolescents need to explore and find answers to the following questions:

What does God think of me?
Who has God called me to become?
What do I do well?
Who do I enjoy being with?
What do I want out of life?
What matters to me?
What kind of person do I want to be?
What is meaningful to me?
What kind of legacy do I want to leave behind?
Who do I want to serve and how can I serve them?

Parents can either stifle or support a teenager's need to discern who God has designed him or her to become. In this chapter, I begin with the greatest obstacle to identity development—status anxiety—and conclude with some practical tips for helping teens develop coherent, stable, and meaningful identities.

Barriers to Identity Development: Status Anxiety

Author and psychotherapist Michael Simon defines status anxiety as the intensive and pervasive worry about whether the world loves you (Simon 2012). It seems that status anxiety may be on the upswing as evidenced by the current popularity of social media sites such as Instagram and Snapchat and TikTok. On these sites, adolescents receive immediate feedback in the form of likes or dislikes as well as comments on how they look, who they are, and what they do. Some adolescents obsessively check the number of followers and/or the number of likes they can generate in order to bolster a fragile sense of self.

Unfortunately, the intense drive to increase status through carefully crafted presentations of oneself on social media disrupts a teenager's ability to connect in face-to-face relationships. This preoccupation with the approval of others on detracts and distracts adolescents from managing daily responsibilities at home and school.

Adolescents who become overly concerned about comparing their lives to others on social media develop what has been termed "Facebook depression." These teens experience emptiness, anxiety, and despondency due to the belief that they cannot live up to the image of others they see portrayed on social media sites. In fact, many teens become depressed because they know they do not even live up to the image of themselves they create on social media.

Fortunately, parents can help impressionable teens by reminding them that, as Christians, they are beloved children of God with unlimited value. Parents can encourage their sons and daughters with the biblical truths that God has made them in His image, has placed extreme worth on their lives, and loves them beyond what they can ever imagine only because of His grace and not because of their works. Finally, parents can explain to teens that their objective status is not determined by the fleeting and fickle standards of the prevailing cultural trends but rather by the immutable, perfect, and loving God of the universe.

In the above sentence, I intentionally use the phrase "objective worth" and not "subjective worth." I say this because teens can *feel* inadequate and insecure (subjective worth), while simultaneously trusting that they have been "fearfully and wonderfully made" (Psalm 139:14) and will be equipped for "the work of ministry" (Ephesians 4:12) that honor and glorify God (objective worth). Parents can remind adolescents that who they are does not depend on how they feel with friends but rather who they are in Christ.

Trusting God for an identity is not an easy task for any adolescent. Because adolescents are highly reactive to emotional states and the acceptance of others, their identities are too often unduly influenced by peers, media, and culture. As important as it is to be aware of one's feelings, it is just as important that adolescents not allow feelings to be the sole determinant of their self-worth.

In my private practice, I encourage teenage clients to feel fully but choose wisely. In my opinion, it is always best to discover and embrace our identities in Christ and to live in alignment with those identities. This means living courageously and often in a counractercultural manner without attachment to the reactions of others. Some parents may believe that this is too much to ask of a teenager. I wholeheartedly disagree. I believe teenagers can step up to the plate and live according to their identities in Christ, especially if they have parents who believe and support their effort.

Promoting Identity Development

Mirroring

The first thing parents can do to promote healthy identity development is mirroring. Mirroring refers to the activity of noticing teens and cheering for them when they invite you to notice and affirm what they are doing. For example, if your teenager asks you to look at a photograph he or she took, a dance he or she choreographed, a new pair of shoes he or she bought, a difficult skateboard trick he or she has mastered, or a creative poem he or she recently wrote, then your teenager is probably looking for a mirroring response. In order to mirror, parents need to communicate interest and admiration for whatever they are seeing. In other words, adolescents value themselves when they receive value from their parents.

Even if your teenager does not directly ask you to see him or her in action, he or she may invite you to mirror him or her in an indirect way. For example, my daughter, Malia, shared with me a few years ago that she felt happy with her college application essays. Although there was no direct request being made, I responded by asking her if I could read them. She agreed, and I showed a sincere interest in her talent for writing and an admiration for the time and effort she put into her essays. After I finished, the smile on her face told me I had succeeded in meeting an important psychological need.

Identification

Identification refers to the sense that our teens feel like us. There is nothing wrong with this process as long as our teens are identifying with a positive aspect of our own identities. Promoting identification may seem counter to the idea of promoting autonomy. However, it is just as important for teens to feel like their parents as it is for them to feel unlike their parents. In other words, it is normal and helpful for your teenager to share some of your best attributes.

Idealization

Idealization is the need for adolescents to admire their parents' positive character traits and accomplishments. Psychological research supports the notion that identity formation correlates with teens who value their parents and see them as successful (Sandhu 2006).

Idealization promotes identity formation for two reasons. First, when teenagers see their parents as successful and strong, it can bolster their self-esteem. Adolescents thrive when they feel respected by a parent they hold in high regard. Second, when parents feel secure and content with their own lives, adolescents feel free to individuate (i.e., independently and responsibly pursue individual interests, activities, relationships, and vocational aspirations).

This means that teenagers benefit when a parent says "thank you" in response to a compliment or affirmation. For example, yesterday after I found out an article I wrote had been published, I spontaneously thought of sharing this news with not only my wife but my children as well. My rationale for sharing the news with my children was that they would enjoy seeing their dad's successes.

Allow Teens to Try on Different Selves

In order to commit to an authentic identity, adolescents first need to explore different paths. A helpful analogy to finding an identity is the process of a teenage girl trying to find just the right dress for the upcoming homecoming dance. In order to know which dress feels best, she may need to try on several dress types, styles, and colors. Parents who promote this process of "trying on different dresses" in life help adolescents grow into their identities. I have seen such a process with my sixteen-year-old son, Blake, who has tried on various sports identities, such as skateboarder, surfer, motocross rider, football quarterback, ice hockey player, and, most recently, fitness fanatic. In addition, his music identity has built up to include hip-hop, R&B, indie, and country. His clothing has evolved from basic casual wear to new high fashion designs.

Get to Know Your Teen Deeply

Getting to know our teens is deeply is helpful in two ways. First, it forces them to reflect on who they are. Second, it sends the message that who they are even in the most vulnerable places has tremendous value to their parents. We accomplish this by maintaining an attitude of curiosity, asking penetrating questions, and listening to understand rather than jumping to conclusions or making false assumptions. Particular topics to explore include our adolescent's interests, skills, and dreams for the future. Below is a short list of great questions parents can ask to get to know their teen better:

> What is important to you?
> How do you think you are gifted?
> What abilities do you want to refine?
> What kind of person do you want to become?
> Who do you want to help in your life?

What kind of difference do you want to make in
the world?
What kind of life do you want to live?

Challenge Your Teen to Think for Themselves

It can help teens increase self-awareness when you ask them what
they think about what they see and experience. In addition, you can
ask them why they think the way they do and how their thinking
reflects their own emerging values.

Encourage Authenticity

Perhaps the best way to encourage authenticity is to live authentic
lives. This means that parents practice what they preach. Teens
are masters at finding hypocrisy, so if parents demand a certain
standard of living, they need to live according to the same criteria.

Parents can also encourage authenticity by affirming their teens
when they see them choosing authentic behavior even when it is
socially unpopular. For instance, in high school my daughter chose
to avoid parties with alcohol because she believed that underage
binge drinking that often occurred at these parties was dangerous
and self-defeating. I was intentional about complimenting her on
this countercultural decision.

Get Involved

As teens pursue activities and experiences that align with their
developing identities, parents can support them by getting involved
in those same activities and experiences. This means that parents
make every effort to attend their adolescent's games, events,
competitions, activities, and performances. It also means playing and
participating in activities your adolescent enjoys. My commitment

to this principle has resulted in my participation in cooking classes, sports of all kinds, board games, hiking, biking, camping, tree climbing, yoga, ice-skating, PlayStation, motorcycle riding, and even dancing. A parent's presence solidifies the comfortability a teen feels with his or her burgeoning self. A parent's participation will give adolescents the necessary confidence to move forward in the process of exploring and achieving an enduring and cohesive sense of self.

Provide Opportunities for Growth

In many cases, providing an opportunity for teens to become the best version of themselves means parents have to make significant personal sacrifices and financial outlays. Private schools, skating lessons, cooking classes, club sport fees, writing camps, church camps, acting workshops, musical instruments, voice lessons, piano lessons, guitar lessons, sports equipment, and travel to game sites all over North America have certainly drained the Mendez family finances over the years. However, the joy of watching our teens thrive has far outweighed any personal sacrifices or financial costs incurred.

Give Them Your Blessing

Finally, it is crucial to give teens a blessing for the identities they achieve through their own process of exploration and commitment. Verbalizing phrases such as "I am proud of you," "I respect you," "I believe in you," and "I love who you are" are extremely uplifting to hear.

Parents know that their adolescent has achieved a coherent and stable identity when their adolescent can articulate a meaningful understanding of him- or herself. I remember when I first knew my daughter, Malia, had achieved a solid identity. I was reading a response she wrote on a college application to the question, "What is your favorite word?" She answered as follows: "My favorite word is Ardent because it epitomizes how I see myself. I am passionate, intensely devoted, vehement and fierce."

As I read this, I began to cry, knowing that the word *ardent* perfectly describes the person God designed Malia to be. I am fully convinced she will use this divinely given character trait to honor and glorify God as she leans into His plans and purposes for her life.

6

AUTONOMY

When I was a child, I spoke like a child, I thought like a child, I reasoned like a child. When I became a man, I gave up childish ways.
— 1 Corinthians 13:11

AUTONOMOUS ADOLESCENTS LIVE in an independent and responsible manner while simultaneously remaining relationally connected to their parents. The development of responsible freedom and the maintenance of close relationships to parents helps adolescents thrive. Recent psychological research has found that parents who support the growth of autonomy are more likely to have adolescents who are less depressed and more self-confident than their peers (Duineveld 2017).

It is crucial to understand that autonomous adolescents are *not* detached from parents (Lamborn and Steinberg 1993). Rather, for adolescents, the healthy transition to independence and responsibility occurs best when parents and adolescents remain interpersonally connected (Ryan and Lynch 1989).

Autonomous adolescents who maintain a strong connection to their parents extend their range of intimate relationships and individual responsibilities. Conversely, detached adolescents often feel overwhelmed, confused, and alone. Autonomous adolescents see their relationship with parents as a secure base from which to explore new ideas, opportunities, and relationships and a safe haven for obtaining support and encouragement.

This chapter examines two types of adolescent autonomy I will refer to as value based and behavioral.

Value-Based Autonomy

Adolescents who achieve value-based autonomy develop their own beliefs and convictions. They make more value-based decisions without the advice and influence of parents. Parents can facilitate this process by staying out of the way as these individualized beliefs and values emerge. This especially applies to beliefs and values adolescents do not share with their parents. When parents discourage independent thinking and decision-making, adolescents will adapt by either accommodating to parental values at the expense of their own development or adhering to personal values while detaching from parents. Either way, adolescents pay a hefty price when parents implicitly or explicitly hinder the development of autonomy.

In order to promote autonomy, parents must identify and clarify adolescents' values rather than determining their values for them. In addition, parents need to encourage adolescents to live in accordance with their newly discovered values. For instance, when my son Brennon was in high school, he did not believe in God and therefore found it incongruent to attend church with our family. Although I prayed for Brennon to become a believer and attend church with our family, I respected his decision to live in alignment with his chosen values by not attending church. The happy ending to this story is that Brennon has placed his faith in God and now freely chooses to attend church with us.

Another example of value-based autonomy was my daughter's decision as an adolescent to abstain from eating meat other than fish. She made this decision because she believed that eating meat supported the practice of animal cruelty. Although she was only twelve at the time, she was resolute with her decision. My wife told her she could do this as long as she prepared her own meals when necessary. Seven years later, at the age of nineteen, my daughter still does not eat meat and has become quite proficient at preparing her own healthy, meatless meals.

Behavioral Autonomy

Behavioral autonomy reflects the capacity to make independent decisions and behave in a responsible manner. This capacity develops through consistent parental support whenever independent decision-making is safe, responsible, and developmentally appropriate. A good rule of thumb I follow is "If teenagers can do it for themselves, then they probably should be doing it for themselves."

Promoting behavioral autonomy can be particularly difficult when adolescents feel a natural desire to spend time away from family members. At times, adolescents may prefer to spend time in their room or in another room of the house separate from other family members. Adolescents may not want to participate in every family activity. It is important for parents to resist making comments that induce guilt when adolescents pull away. If parents subtly or not so subtly succumb to guilt-inducing behaviors, they will likely promote what psychologists have termed *separation guilt*. Adolescents who feel separation guilt will often give up normal autonomous strivings in order to avoid hurting their parents' feelings.

Teenagers can demonstrate behavioral autonomy in a multitude of ways, such as preferences in music, media, clothing, school classes, extracurricular activities, and choice of friends. How teens spend their time and money, where they choose to work, and how often they choose to study, exercise, or socialize can all reflect a budding sense of autonomy.

Parents can promote behavioral autonomy by accepting the personal preferences of their teenagers. For instance, a few years ago, I took my daughter to a motorcycle equipment store to buy her some new off-road riding gear. My only stipulation was that she buy all the equipment necessary to keep her safe. However, when it came to style, color, brand, or fit, I left the decision entirely up to her. I saw this shopping spree as a wonderful opportunity to promote behavioral autonomy. As I expected, she chose brands, colors, and styles much different than I would have chosen for her. However, to my surprise, she also chose less expensive items than I would have chosen, and my commitment to supporting her autonomy ended up saving me money!

Respecting behavioral autonomy does not mean that parents permit teens to make dangerous decisions. For example, I never allow my son to ride his skateboard without a helmet. I never allow my daughter to walk by herself on campus late at night. I never allow any of my children to go on dirt bike rides without a riding companion. I will talk more about the need for adolescents to be remain safe in the next chapter.

Promoting behavioral autonomy also does not mean giving your adolescent permission to skip responsibilities in order to pursue independence. For instance, last week, Blake asked my wife and me on Friday if he could take a spontaneous trip with his friends to Big Bear Lake for the upcoming weekend. I reminded him that he had already committed to attending hockey practice on Saturday. He asked if he could miss practice to go on the trip. I said no because it was his responsibility to follow through on his commitments.

I am comfortable allowing my children to make decisions that may result in temporary pain. For instance, two years ago, Blake decided that he was going to spend his entire supply of cash at a "supreme" clothing store he asked to visit on our vacation to New

York City. His rationale for spending so much money was that he could resale whatever he bought to his friends at twice his purchase price. I privately feared that his friends might not follow through with their commitment to purchasing his items. However, I kept my feelings to myself, believing that such a remark might inadvertently convey that I was not in favor of Blake spending his money as he chose. Instead, I told him I was impressed with his entrepreneurial spirit. As it turns out, he ended up selling some of the items at a price below his cost due to some of his prospective buyers reneging on their initial promises. This was a painful learning process for Blake but not a harmful one. He learned a valuable lesson about the relationship between risk and return in the business world. More importantly, he remained assured that I respect and support his new ideas and ventures.

Another example of an autonomy test occurred just after I bought a preowned Honda CRF 250R motorcycle for my then fourteen-year-old son, Blake. As with all used dirt bikes, this one was not without issues. One of the issues was that it was difficult to kick-start at the beginning of a riding trip. I vividly remember the simultaneous look of determination and despair on Blake's face as he kicked and kicked without success the first time we took the bike out to the desert. I recall desperately wanting to take over and kick-start the bike for him, but I knew that would not be wise. Instead, I watched and prayed that Blake's next kick would do the job. After several attempts, the Honda eventually roared to life. My exhausted son had the sweetest and sweatiest smile I have ever seen. It was a priceless moment.

A confusing example of an autonomy test is adolescent arguing. Most parents agree that adolescents frequently argue. It may come as a surprise, but this phenomenon is not necessarily a reflection of disrespect. Rather, sometimes adolescents disagree and argue in order to bolster growing need for a separate and cohesive sense of self. In other words, disagreeing and arguing allows adolescents to feel distinct from their parents. Sometimes when adolescents disagree, they may actually be making a good point, and it is helpful to allow them to influence your thinking and behavior. Other times, they may argue in support of a perspective you absolutely disagree with on moral, logical, factual, or practical grounds. When this happens, it is wise to agree to disagree. Either of these approaches will calm your adolescent and help him or her to feel comfortable thinking differently even when he or she disagrees with your point of view.

Unwelcomed Behavioral Autonomy

Life would be easier if adolescents welcomed every opportunity to function in an autonomous fashion. Unfortunately, this is not reality. Adolescents sometimes resist independent functioning even when doing so would be in their best interests. Completing chores, filling out school forms, scheduling appointments, cleaning the bedroom and bathroom, doing laundry, keeping a calendar, keeping commitments, getting a job, and making meals are all common examples of necessary but unwanted autonomy. I often joke with my wife that adolescents want to be independent where they should be dependent and dependent where they should be independent. Promoting unwelcome behavioral autonomy means that parents require adolescents to do what they can and should do for themselves.

For example, one morning, my then high school daughter, Malia, asked my wife to clean up our outdoor courtyard. Malia explained to my wife that she had spontaneously decided on the day of her interview with an admissions representative from Princeton that it would be more comfortable to have the conversation outdoors. Understandably, my wife was dismayed that my daughter had made this request at the last minute. She then lamented to me how much work it would take to make the courtyard area presentable. Bikes needed to move to the garage. Dog poop needed to be picked up. Trash barrels needed relocation. The patio table needed cleaning, and the concrete ground needed a water rinse. Fortunately, my wife quickly realized that this was a wonderful opportunity to give my daughter some unwelcomed autonomy. She admirably and calmly asked Malia to handle the necessary prep work for her impromptu outdoor experience. To our surprise, Malia complied without protest and did an excellent job cleaning and straightening the area. The funny thing about this story is that Malia ended up doing the interview in the house. We said nothing about this to Malia, knowing that even allowing her to change her mind was also a way of promoting autonomy.

This previous example reminds me of an interesting phenomenon I have witnessed as a psychotherapist. I have consistently found that although teens may consciously protest and passively resist engaging in unwelcome autonomous behavior, they unconsciously crave it. I am convinced that adolescents unconsciously hope that parents will resist the urge to do things for them they can do for themselves even when they consciously protest. Conversely, adolescents often become progressively more irritable, disrespectful, and downright mean-spirited when their parents become more "helpful." I believe this poor attitude is an adolescent's unconscious way of expressing the displeasure of a failed autonomy test. Sadly, I have worked with many bewildered and resentful parents who cannot comprehend how disrespectful their teen has become when these parents have "worked so hard" to do "so much" for their teenager. My advice to these exasperated parents is simple. Do less! Hence, I often say things like "Stop making lunch for your kid," or "Let them do their own laundry." Amazingly, when parents follow my advice, they often find their teens becoming more kind and respectful.

Practical Tips for Promoting Autonomy

There are several practical ways parents can help adolescents become more autonomous. Below is a list of suggestions:

- Get comfortable with adolescents not wanting affection from you in public places.
- Get comfortable with adolescents not wanting to walk with you in public places.
- Give adolescents a private place to hang out alone or with their friends in your house.
- Allow adolescents to have negative feelings even if they do not make sense.
- Model comfortability with autonomous behavior.
- Ask adolescents what they think or feel an issue or topic.
- If an adolescent says no, do not try to change it to a yes.
- Trust adolescents will often find good enough solutions on their own.
- Allow adolescents to influence your decisions and behavior.
- Avoid putting adolescents on guilt trips for preferring or valuing something different than you.
- Do not fight battles for adolescents they can handle on their own.
- Avoid giving adolescents unsolicited advice.
- Do not control how adolescents spend money (give them an allowance).

Passing Autonomy Tests

One of the most important ways parents can help adolescents is to pass what I call autonomy tests. Autonomy tests may sometimes be conscious but usually are unconscious attempts aimed at challenging the unconscious fear that it is not safe to grow up. When parents pass autonomy tests, adolescents win. These fortunate adolescents take more risks, feel more confidence in themselves, and vigorously pursue their passions and dreams. Autonomy tests come in many shapes and sizes. It takes a wise and discerning parent to recognize and pass these types of unconscious tests.

For example, my daughter, Malia, presented an autonomy test when she was a high school student. We had scheduled a motorcycle-riding trip on an upcoming weekend. Everyone in our family was excited about this trip, including Malia, who had recently purchased all new riding gear. However, Malia found out the week before the trip that her boyfriend was competing in the CIF playoffs on the same weekend. This put Malia in a quandary. "Do I go with my family and let my boyfriend down, or do I support my boyfriend and let my family down?" Not only was she conflicted about her decision, she was also afraid of making the "wrong" choice. Malia asked me what she should do. I saw this as an autonomy test. In order to pass the test, I did three things. First, I told Malia that she needed to make her own decision. Second, I told her that I would be disappointed but not devastated if she chose not to go riding. Finally, I told her that I would fully support whatever decision she made. She decided not to go riding, but she also asked if I could plan another motorcycle-riding trip as soon as possible. I happily agreed to her request and affirmed her for making this tough decision on her own.

Autonomy tests are not always easy to discern and/or pass. One of my most difficult autonomy tests occurred when my then eighth-grade son, Blake, informed me that he no longer wanted to play competitive ice hockey. I have to admit this was not disappointing but rather devastating (although I did not share that with him). I also need to confess that I initially did not handle this news well at all. I foolishly put Blake on a guilt trip by reminding him how much time and money I had invested in his hockey career. Fortunately, the Holy Spirit clearly and strongly convicted me that I was in the wrong. When I came to my senses, I recognized this as an autonomy test. I told Blake that after he finished out his current season, he had my blessing to hang up his skates for good, and I apologized for my immature response. Thankfully, Blake accepted my apology.

After Blake's retirement, he spent a great deal of time and effort honing his skills as a quarterback through twice-weekly lessons and playing competitive flag football. He spent more time riding his dirt bike and body boarding at the beach. He signed up for a summer junior lifeguard program. I remember watching his quarterback lessons and Friday-night flag football games with mixed emotions. I wanted to honor his autonomous choices in life, but I was also grieving the end of his hockey career.

The next year, something unexpected happened. Blake independently decided to play for his high school ice hockey team. He unretired from hockey. Currently, he plays both Tier 1 club hockey and high school ice hockey. He is hoping to play at the Division 1 college level. Throughout this process, I have seen the Lord's hand at work. I am reminded of my favorite verse from the book of Proverbs: "Trust in the Lord with all your heart, and do not lean on your own understanding, in all your ways acknowledge Him and he will make your paths straight" (Proverbs 3:5–6). I firmly believe the Lord wanted me to trust my son's capacity to find his own path in life.

PROTECTION

He will cover you with his pinions, and under his wings you will find refuge; his faithfulness is a shield and buckler.

—Psalm 91:4

This God—his way is perfect; the word of the Lord proves true; he is a shield for all those who take refuge in him.

—2 Samuel 22:31

JUST AS CHRISTIANS desire the safekeeping of their heavenly Father, adolescents hunger and thirst for parental protection. Although teens rarely explicitly ask for protection, it is one of their most important psychological needs. Because the prefrontal cortex of the teenage brain responsible for higher-level thinking is not finished developing until the age of twenty-five, parents of adolescents may need to intervene when their teenager is on the precipice of a dangerous decision or pondering participation in a risky activity.

Psychological research confirms an adolescent's need for protection. Haase (2008) has found that premature curfew autonomy correlates with lower subjective well-being in late adolescence. Matza, Kupersmidt, and Glenn (2001) found that rejected adolescents reported lower levels of "parental monitoring" by both parents. Psychologists describe parental monitoring as "parental awareness, watchfulness and supervision of adolescent activities in multiple domains such as friends, school and behavior at home and communication to the adolescent that the parent is concerned about and aware of those activities" (Dishion and McMahon 1998). What psychologists refer to as parental monitoring I would call parental protection.

In order to protect adolescents, parents need to understand that adolescents are very adept at asking for what they unconsciously hope their parents will *not* give them. In other words, adolescents may seem very convincing in their requests to put themselves in harm's way when what they really want is a parent who will say no. It is wise for parents to remember the words of Proverbs 20:5: "The purpose in a man's heart is like deep water." In other words, teens often do things for reasons outside of their conscious awareness. Conscientious parents utilize biblical stories and accounts of God's consistent practice of shielding His children from danger as an example to emulate as they strive to safeguard their own children.

Parents who value protection must discern when and how to protect their teens. It is crucial to not yield to the prevailing cultural trends or the common practices of other parents. It can be helpful to remember that even in the New Testament, Christians are referred to as "sojourners and exiles" in this world (1 Peter 2:11). Therefore, Christian parents should not be surprised when secular parents view their protective behaviors as excessive and overbearing.

Barriers to Protection

The biggest barrier to protection is the false belief that whatever an adolescent requests is what he or she needs. This common misconception often leads to parents failing what I term protection tests. It is important to note that a protection test is usually an unconscious process. In other words, adolescents may convincingly ask for a yes and consciously hope for a yes while unconsciously hoping for a no.

For example, when my son Blake was thirteen, he loved to ride his skateboard with his neighborhood friends, learning and practicing new tricks. I remember one particular day when I saw Blake take off with his friends without wearing his helmet. I told him he always needed to wear his helmet when riding his skateboard. His reaction was predictable. He replied, "But, Dad, none of my friends are wearing helmets. If I am the only kid wearing a helmet, I will I feel like a total loser. Trust me, Dad. I'm not going to fall and crack my head open." This is a common example of a teen overtly asking for one thing but unconsciously desiring another. I calmly responded, "I understand you don't want to feel embarrassed with your friends, but because I care about your safety, you always need to wear your helmet when you ride your skateboard." I added, "So you need to put on your helmet now. And if I ever see you skateboarding without a helmet, you will lose the privilege of riding your skateboard for a week."

My response is what I would call passing the protection test. On the other hand, I could have failed this protection test if I said something shaming such as, "Fine, if you want to be reckless, go for it, but if you fall and hurt yourself, remember that I told you so." I could also fail the protection test by placing too much faith in my son's judgment by saying something like, "OK fine, but please be careful." I could also fail this test if I said something guilt inducing like, "Fine. Have it your way, but know your mother will be devastated if you end up hurting yourself." All the above ways of failing this protection test probably sound familiar. However, the truth is that they all fail to meet a teenager's deep need for protection.

Promoting Protection

There are many ways to protect teens from harm, and they all require extra work for parents. However, this extra work is well worth the effort. Here is a sample list of ideas:

> *Monitor your teen.* Know where he or she is, what he or she is doing and with whom he or she is hanging out. Get names and phone numbers of your teen's friends and their parents.

> *Meet the parents of your teen's friends.* Clearly communicate to other parents your desire to protect your adolescent. Most parents will appreciate this.

> *Maximize the time your teen spends in the midst of responsible adult supervision.* This may mean making your home a welcoming place for your teen's friends so you can provide responsible adult supervision. Make sure you have a good supply of tasty food and refreshing drinks. Provide comfortable spaces for teens to hang out in your home, yard, or garage. Get to know your teenager's friends and affirm them liberally so they will enjoy their visit.

> *Avoid overly permissive teachers and coaches.* Watch out for teachers and coaches who are more interested in pleasing and being popular than maintaining a safe environment. It is perfectly fine to remove

your teen from these situations whenever possible, even if your teen protests.

Keep your teen clear of dangerous environments. Refuse requests from your teen to attend social events and parties where there is no responsible adult supervision, especially if alcohol and drugs may be present.

Monitor your teen's social media activity. This does not mean reading every single email or text, but it does mean random checks of emails and texts and regular access to all Instagram, Snapchat, and TikTok accounts. It also means prohibiting access to sites you believe are dangerous.

Reinforce self-protective choices. Catch your teen making wise choices that result in self-protection and affirm them immediately with praise and admiration.

Provide cover stories. This will allow your teen to save face when he or she says no to a potentially dangerous activity. Your teen may feel relief in knowing that he or she always has the option of saying, "I would love to go to the party, but my parents won't let me."

A Sample Protection Test

Last summer, on our family vacation to Maui, we all decided to take an afternoon hike near Paia to check out some beautiful waterfalls and swim in some natural pools along the trail. When we arrived at the final pool, we saw a few adolescents jumping from the top ledge of the waterfall into the pool several feet below. They seemed to be having a great time. Of course, as soon as Blake and Malia saw these young Hawaiian daredevils, they immediately made a beeline for the upper ledge. I wondered to myself if this was safe and whether or not I should stop them. I concluded to myself that it would be safe for Malia and Blake to jump in as long as they left from the same spot on the upper ledge and landed in the same spot in the pool as the Hawaiian adolescents. In this instance, I believe I passed the autonomy test by allowing them to jump but also passed the protection test by insisting they only jump and land in the same places as the native Hawaiian adolescents.

Final Comments

Passing protection tests is sometimes easy and sometimes difficult. It always involves discernment and careful consideration of the context and the individual teenager. In other words, passing a protection test is always case specific. The good news is that if parents fail a protection test, their adolescent will simply continue to test, hoping his or her parents will eventually pass.

Passing protection tests does not always mean going against the stated request of your teen. Sometimes teens consciously and unconsciously want the same thing. For instance, a few years ago on a family dirt bike–riding trip, I asked my then sixteen-year-old daughter, Malia, if she would like to lead on our afternoon ride in order to stop eating dirt from my bike. I was thinking that she would appreciate this kind gesture and accept my invitation with relief and gratitude. Her response surprised me. She asked if she could stay behind me. I saw her request as a protection test. She felt unsafe leading the ride. Maybe she was afraid of getting lost or not noticing a dangerous section on the trail. I agreed to lead the ride, and she seemed relieved. In this instance, I passed her protection test by complying with her request.

Interestingly, my then fourteen-year-old son, Blake, asked me if he could lead on the same ride. I did not see his request as a protection test but rather an autonomy test, given his level of skill and confidence. I said, "Go for it," and passed his autonomy test. This story demonstrates how the same request can represent a protection test for one child and an autonomy test for another child.

8

ACCEPTANCE

I ask then, has God rejected his people? By no means!
—Romans 11:1

THE OLD TESTAMENT is replete with story after story of God's unrelenting pursuit of His children despite their frequent rejection of Him. These biblical narratives show that God's favor is not dependent on the dedication and devotion of His children. Rather, God's love for His children undeserved and unconditional. Although we often turn our backs on Him, God will never turn His back on us. The writer of Hebrews puts it this way: "I will never leave you nor forsake you" (Hebrews 13:5).

God's unconditional acceptance is an excellent example of how we can best love our adolescents. When we satisfy our teenagers' deepest thirst for unconditional love and acceptance, we abide in the biblical mandate to not "provoke" (Ephesians 6:4) our children. A firm commitment to loving teens despite rejection and defiance creates and sustains an adolescent's feelings of security, safety, and overall well-being.

Psychological research substantiates both the personal and relational benefits of parental acceptance, as well as the negative consequences of parental rejection. Amato and Ochiltree (1986) found that parental rejection correlates with both anxiety and depression. Fauber (1990) found that parental rejection correlates with serious behavioral problems in adolescence. On the other hand, parental acceptance is associated with positive outcomes in adolescents such as intimacy, mutual respect, and reciprocal admiration (Sinha 2007).

Barriers to Acceptance

The most common barrier to parental acceptance is the common practice of responding to perceived rejection with rejection. Notice, that I said *perceived rejection*. In my experience, when parents interpret their teens' behaviors as outright rejection, what is often really happening is that their teen is simply trying to meet an autonomy need such as independence, separation, and/or privacy. Furthermore, when adolescents pursue legitimate needs that parents interpret as rejection, parents often end up feeling dismissed, unimportant, and ultimately unloved. Parents often reflexively respond to these feelings by hurting back. This retaliation can come in the form of overt hostility, covert guilt trips, or silent detachment.

When parents retaliate, they say or do things that feel profoundly rejecting to their teen. Parental rejection can be conveyed through verbal comments, nonverbal gestures, and/or distancing behaviors. Parental rejection in any form crushes a teenager's spirit. The Bible speaks to this saying, "A soft answer turns away wrath, but a harsh word stirs up anger" (Proverbs 15:1). In addition, the Bible teaches us that "there is one whose rash words are like sword thrusts, but the tongue of the wise brings healing" (Proverbs 12:18). Below are some common phrases that pierce an adolescent's heart like a sword:

- "Why are you so mean to me?"
- "Stop being so rude."
- "It hurts my feelings when you don't want to be around me or our family."
- "What is wrong with you?"
- "It seems like I can't even have a normal conversation with you."
- "You never talk to me anymore."
- "Am I really that bad of a parent that you can't be seen in public with me?"
- "If you don't want to be a part of this family, why don't you leave?"
- "Why do you push me away when I'm just trying to help you?"
- "After all I have done for you, how can you be so ungrateful?"
- "I don't deserve to be treated like this."

In addition, scripture speaks directly to the importance of resisting the temptation to respond to an injury without retaliation. Jesus said, "If anyone slaps you on the right cheek, turn to him the other also" (Matthew 5:39). Romans says, "Beloved, never avenge yourselves, but leave it to the wrath of God, for it is written, 'Vengeance is mine, I will repay, says the Lord.'" (Romans 12:19). Below are some common examples of retaliatory actions:

- ignoring your teen after feeling ignored by him or her
- refusing affection after your teen has refused affection
- not inviting your teen to participate in family activities after he or she has declined a previous invitation
- giving short answers after your teen has given you short answers

- avoiding interactions in the home with your teen after feeling ignored
- telling your teen you are too busy to be involved in his or her activities or to drive him or her to the activities after feeling that he or she has not made time for you

All of the above words and actions only serve to deflate an adolescent's spirit. In order to prevent this destructive pattern, I ask parents I work with in my private practice to do two things. First, do not take it personally when you feel rejected by your adolescent. Remind yourself that your adolescent loves you. Adolescents may be rejecting at times, but they continue to need the patient availability and presence of their parents. Second, I ask parents to feel fully but choose wisely. In other words, I ask them to stop, breathe, and nonjudgmentally pay attention to their own feelings. Then I ask parents to identify and enact a wise and loving response.

A common example can illustrate what I mean by this second directive. Suppose your teenager turns away as you gently and affectionately put your arm around him or her. In this moment, you will likely feel rejected, hurt, and maybe even angry. It is important to validate your feelings rather than beating yourself up for experiencing negative emotions. There is nothing wrong with you. Next, instead of behaving automatically according to your impulses, take a few deep breaths and ask yourself what a wise choice would look like. In this case, a wise choice would be gently moving your arm away without saying any hurtful words or engaging in any provocative actions. Later, when your teen inevitably seeks out affection, respond in kind, even though you may still be feeling some residue of resentment.

Promoting Acceptance

Passing Rejection Tests

The above illustration is an example of what I call passing a rejection test. A rejection test is a conscious or sometimes unconscious maneuver by your teen to first reject you and then, at a later point in time, seek out your acceptance. Parents can pass rejection tests by responding with wisdom and unconditional acceptance rather than emotion and impulse. Rejection tests are difficult to pass because adolescents need a parental response that is counterintuitive. Below is another example of a rejection test.

On a car ride home from hockey practice, I asked Blake if he was planning to buy Christmas presents for his family and girlfriend. He sarcastically replied, "No I'm not getting anybody anything." I then asked him if he needed my help with coming up with ideas or driving him to any stores. He brusquely responded, "I'm fine." He then remained quiet. I attended to my feelings, which included frustration, rejection, and resentment. After all, I was trying to be helpful, and he practically bit my head off. I thought it would be a nice time to have a conversation about Christmas presents, and he preferred to keep his thoughts to himself. Five minutes later, Blake asked me for advice about how to study for final exams. This was clearly a rejection test. Five minutes after he had clearly rejected my insight, he was now asking for my help. I felt a strong urge to ignore him or tell him he needed to learn how to study for finals himself. Fortunately, I knew that responding in this manner would fail his rejection test. I answered his question with a thoughtful and gentle response. He seemed quite relieved and actually agreed to take my advice. His decision to allow my influence and his nonverbal signs of relief indicated to me that I had just passed a difficult rejection test.

Interestingly, the following day, Blake presented me with a second rejection test. He asked me what I thought he should buy his girlfriend for Christmas. This totally caught me off guard. I noticed that I felt an impulse to say something foolish such as, "Well, yesterday it seemed like you had this whole Christmas gift thing under control and didn't want my help, so I'm sure you can figure it out." Fortunately, I did not. Instead, I chose wisely, giving him various ideas on what types of gifts I thought would be both meaningful to his girlfriend as well as budget friendly.

A more recent rejection test occurred when I asked Blake if he wanted to see an action-adventure movie with me I thought he would enjoy. He said no because he did not want to be seen with his dad at the theater I had recommended. He told me that many of his friends hang out at the entertainment center where the movie was playing. I felt hurt and rejected that I was making an effort to connect with my son and he was refusing my invitation. This especially stung because, as a child, I would have liked nothing more than for my father to invite me to the movies with him. Five minutes later, I heard Blake yelling from upstairs, "Dad, can we see the movie at a different theater?" I felt like saying no. I was deeply hurt, partly by Blake but mostly because Blake had touched an old childhood wound. I felt fully and responded wisely, as I agreed to check out other theaters. Test passed.

This example is a bit more complicated because the difficulty of this test was rooted in a childhood injury. God helped me recognize this, which made it easier to respond to Blake in a helpful manner. In the same way, I recommend to parents that they look out for rejection tests that touch wounds from childhood.

My daughter, Malia, presented an interesting rejection test a few years ago. She was invited to speak about her summer camp experience at her high school youth group Sunday-morning service. That morning, she casually asked me if I had planned to come watch her speak. Fortunately, I speak the adolescent language and translated her question as "I would love you to come watch me speak. It would mean the world to me. Can you please come?" Based on my translation, I attended the service, making sure to stand in the back corner. My daughter was delighted to see me show up and even gave me a hug in front of her friends before the service started. This was all the confirmation I needed to know I had passed her unconscious rejection test.

Enthusiastic Responses to Bids

A second way to promote acceptance is to respond positively and enthusiastically to adolescents' unprompted bids for connection, affirmation, and validation. Examples of these conversations are:

Malia: "Do you like the dress I bought?"
Dad: "Oh yeah, it's amazing! It totally fits your style."

Blake: "Did you see the move I made before I scored the goal?"
Dad: "I sure did. That was an awesome toe drag. You nailed it!"

Malia: "Mom I need you." (Snuggles with Mom.)
Mom: "I love you, sissy. Stay here for a bit and keep me warm."

Blake: "Hey, Dad, can we watch our show?"
Dad: "Absolutely. I can't wait to see what happens next."

Supporting Hopes and Dreams

A third way of promoting acceptance is to support the hopes and dreams of your adolescent.

Blake is hoping to play ice hockey for Princeton University. This is a lofty goal and a big dream. The best thing I can say to Blake is that I believe that he is capable of doing this, and I will do everything in my power to help him achieve his dream. The worst thing I can say is that he has no idea how difficult it is to play at such an elite level and that he should be more realistic and understand that very few players get accepted to such a prestigious academic institution.

Along the same vein, my daughter, Malia, often questions her decision to major in English in hopes of becoming a writer. She wonders if she should have chosen a more practical major and career path. My approach with her is similar. I tell her that I truly believe she is a gifted writer and that she can make a career out of being an author. Even though she responds with a dismissive look of disbelief due to what she terms my "Daddy bias," I am convinced that my response has a positive impact on her desire to pursue her passion.

Accepting All Feelings

A final way to show acceptance to adolescents is to validate rather than challenge both positive and negative feelings. In Romans, Paul echoes this sentiment saying, "Rejoice with those who rejoice, weep with those who weep" (Romans 12:15) This means that when your adolescent is excited, you respond in kind rather than bursting his or her bubble in the name of promoting humility. If adolescents scream with joy, then you scream too. If they dance, then you dance. Let them fully enjoy their positive feelings.

On the other hand, when your teen is feeling down, it is best to avoid the temptation to cheer them up. No parent wants to see his or her son or daughter suffer. However, speaking words of cheer without validating painful feelings can leave your teenager feeling alone, misunderstood, and subsequently more frustrated and depressed. Oftentimes, adolescents respond to this approach by suppressing their true feelings and feigning happiness in order to accommodate what they believe their parents need. This pattern becomes a vicious cycle that progressively leads to more isolation and despair. Proverbs affirms the futility of this approach:

"Whoever sings songs to a heavy heart is like one who takes off a garment on a cold day, and like vinegar on soda" (Proverbs 25:20). Therefore, phrases such as "Don't worry," "Cheer up," "Look at the bright side," or "Count your blessings" do not help. Examples of helpful phrases include "I can see how difficult this is for you," "You seem very sad about this," "It makes perfect sense to me how much this hurts," and "I'll bet you felt very angry." In other words, psychological health does not mean that your adolescent has a perpetual smile and always feels happy. Rather, an adolescent's health and well-being positively correlates with the degree to which he or she feels comfortable accessing and expressing the full range of human emotions.

9

COMMUNITY

And let us consider how to stir up one another to love and good works, not neglecting to meet together, as is the habit of some, but encouraging one another and all the more as you see the Day drawing near.

—Hebrews 10:24–25

THE IMPORTANCE OF community for adolescents cannot be overstated. An adolescent's community includes immediate family, extended family, adult friends, and especially same-age friends. A well-known African proverb wisely states, "It takes a village to raise a child." The Bible wholeheartedly affirms the benefits of living this way. The psalmist writes, "Behold, how good and pleasant it is when brothers dwell in unity" (Psalm 133:1). Paul says it this way: "I therefore, a prisoner for the Lord, urge you to walk in a manner worthy of the calling to which you have been called, with all humility and gentleness, with patience, bearing with one another in love, *eager to maintain the unity of the Spirit in the bond of peace*" (Ephesians 4:3).

Community relationships allow adolescents to know and to feel known. Having a sense of community membership provides adolescents with an all-important feeling of belonging. Community promotes safety, security, and significance. Community is the cure for common adolescent feelings of loneliness and isolation. The Bible affirms this, saying, "It is not good that the man should be alone" (Genesis 2:18).

Psychological and sociological research affirms the value of community. Research has found a positive correlation between a sense of community and social well-being among adolescents (Albanesi 2007). In addition, researchers have discovered that an adolescent's sense of connectedness to his or her peers protects him or her from an array of health risk behaviors, including substance use, risky sexual behavior, and violence (Bernat and Resnick 2009). Connectedness also increases an adolescent's sympathy for others, academic success (Anderman and Freeman 2004), and overall psychological well-being (Laible, Carlo, and Raffaelli 2000).

Friendships

An important part of an adolescent's community is his or her friends. Parents become aware of this as they witness their adolescents seeking out increasing amounts of time with friends. According to research, the average American adolescent spends over half their waking hours with peers, as opposed to only 15 percent with adults (Dijkstra and Veenstra 2011). These findings align with other research, which has found that adolescents consider the time they spend with friends as among the most enjoyable parts of their day (Csikszentmihalyi and Larson 1984).

Why are friendships so important? There are several reasons. Friendships provide a setting for adolescents to develop social skills, such as how to be a good friend, how to communicate effectively, how to be a leader, how to respect confidences, how to be vulnerable, and how to build intimacy and mutual trust. In addition, friends provide helpful feedback with regard to identity, and friends significantly influence self-esteem. Furthermore, friendships help adolescents in the development of autonomy and provide a context for the honing of decision-making skills.

Positive friendships promote the psychological well-being of adolescents. For instance, research has found that adolescents who have high academic success typically have friends who have similar academic values and aspirations (Veronneau and Dishion 2011). Furthermore, the academic success of friends not only promotes an adolescent's success in school but also correlates with a lack of involvement in delinquent behavior (Cook, Deng, and Morgano 2007).

Conversely, adolescents with more antisocial friends are more likely to engage in antisocial activity (Criss et al. 2016). The book of Proverbs puts it this way: "Whoever walks with the wise becomes wise, but the companion of fools will suffer harm" (Proverbs 13:20). My sixteen-year-old son's ice hockey coach, Ryan Frost, affirmed this principle when he said to Blake, "Surround yourself with people who support your upward aim."

Adult Friendships

Adult friendships can be just as important as same-age friendships. Adults can offer wisdom and guidance that can only come from years of personal experience. Adults support, encourage, and reaffirm values and beliefs parents have been stressing throughout an adolescent's life. In addition, adult friends connect with adolescents over shared avocations, leisure activities, and personal interests. For instance, my son Blake has formed a bond with my friend Andrew because of a shared passion for surfing. My daughter, Malia, has connected with my wife's friend Kim over a shared interest in media and entertainment. My son Aaron has a connection with my friend Matt through automobiles, and my son Brennon has a shared a love of all things food and cooking with my sister-in-law Lori.

I remember a specific instance when an adult relationship meant the world to me. I was in the eighth grade, and my flag football team had just lost the Torrance city championship game 42–40. I remember being on the verge of tears when Coach John Razzano, from the team we had defeated in the semifinals, approached me after the game. He told me that in all his years of coaching, he had never seen a quarterback performance as good as mine. I will never forget those words and the positive impact they had on my self-esteem. Anytime an adolescent teenage boy hears from an admired and respected adult in his community words to the effect of "You have what it takes," it is a real game changer.

The Role of Parents in Friendships

Parents can help their adolescents by monitoring existing friendships and gently guiding adolescents toward wise, responsible, and well-adjusted friends. One way of doing this is to classify friends into three categories: A, B, and C. "A" friends are those who parents know and respect. Parents also know and respect their parents. Parents can encourage these friendships wholeheartedly. "B" friends are those new friends parents do not yet know well. Parents can allow social activities with these friends as long as it seems safe. Finally, "C" friends are those whom parents deem to be unwise and unsafe. It is wise to prohibit any association with C friends in order to protect your adolescent from potential harm.

Parents encourage healthy friendships by creating warm and welcoming spaces for adolescents to hang out. It is wise to give adolescents a separate space in the home where they can have privacy. It is also a good idea to make your home comfortable and enjoyable for your adolescent's friends. It is helpful to take an interest in the lives of your adolescent's friends, without being too smothering or intrusive. Pray for them, listen to their stories sagas and dramas, and frequently affirm them with positive words and gestures. Invite your adolescent's friends to be part of fun, exciting, and enjoyable activities with your family. Finally, provide a never-ending supply of delicious food and refreshing beverages.

A final way to support a teen's friendships is to teach and model the character traits that will make adolescents a more desirable friend. Psychological research has identified the following traits as correlated with high-quality friendships: warmth, friendliness, sense of humor, compassion, and generosity (Litwack, Aikins, and Cillessen 2012). A second benefit to modeling these positive traits is that adolescents are likely to select friends who resemble parents. Therefore, wise parents attempt to *be* the type of person they want to *see* their adolescents select as a friend. Research confirms this notion, having found that the quality of the relationship between a parent and an adolescent positively correlates with an adolescent's friendship quality and subjective well-being (Chai et al. 2016).

Barriers to Community

Solitary Activities

This includes video games, television, computers, iPads, smartphones, and other solitary activities that are captivating to the point that adolescents fail to maintain a balance between face-to-face interactions and screen time. There is no need to prohibit these solitary pursuits; however, it is important to monitor them and to make sure they are not impeding your adolescent's social development.

Enmeshed Families

Enmeshed families have diffuse boundaries between family members and rigid boundaries between the immediate family and the outside world. These families overemphasize the need for family togetherness at the expense of friendships and healthy contact with the outside community. It is difficult to tell where one family member ends and the other begins. In the enmeshed family system, there is intrusiveness, a lack of privacy, and a lack of personal space. Family members speak for one another and become agitated when one person expresses a different thought, feeling, or perception. These families spend an inordinate amount of time together on weekends and evenings, regardless of the age or developmental stage of the children. When adolescents from an enmeshed family expresses a healthy desire to get out of the family bubble, they often feel guilty and disloyal.

Promoting Community

Below is a list of ideas for parents looking for ways to enrich their adolescent's community:

- Send them to camps with other like-minded adolescents. (We sent our daughter, Malia, to a poetry and creative writing camp when she was in high school.)
- Sign your teen up for church small groups, activities, and outings.
- Drive your teen and pay for extracurricular activities without complaining.
- Schedule family activities with other families where adult-to-adolescent interactions can occur.

I will never forget the surprising words I heard from my then thirteen-year-old son, Blake, while driving him home from his junior high ministry life group. I asked him if it was becoming too much of a burden to continue to attend life group since it took place on a school night. He quickly turned toward me and stated with a full assurance, "Dad, there are two things I look forward to every week: my hockey game and my life group." His words reaffirmed the tremendous value of a small community of friends in the life of an adolescent.

Romantic Relationships

A special type of friendship adolescents may desire and experience is a romantic relationship. Parents are often perplexed when it comes to coping with a lovestruck teen. In response to this, I have developed a list of helpful dating guidelines parents can share with their adolescent.

General Guidelines for Dating

Do not be in a hurry to date. Teenagers who engage in one-on-one dating before the age of sixteen are more likely to have higher rates of behavioral problems.

Do not date someone you would not want to be your friend. Friendship is the foundation for a successful dating relationship.

Do not date a nonbeliever. It is just as likely that an adolescent will fall away from his or her Christian faith as it is he or she will lead a romantic partner to faith in Christ. Hence, Paul's admonition to "not be unequally yoked with unbelievers" (2 Corinthians 6:14).

Do not date for the wrong reasons. If your son or daughter believes that entering into a dating relationship will bring them higher self-esteem and less loneliness, tell them to think again. Oftentimes, adolescents who date romantically find themselves cut off from other friendships, which can actually result in a loss of self-esteem and an increase in loneliness.

Do not isolate from friends and family when you are dating. If your teen chooses to date, make sure he or she nurtures other relationships with friends and family.

Do not let your relationship get in the way of the development of your God-given abilities and gifts. If your son's or daughter's romantic relationship is not growth promoting because of jealously, envy, dependency, or outright selfishness, it is time to get out.

Do not confuse the tingles for real love. The feeling of love can wax and wane. When teens say, "I will always love you," to their romantic interests, what they are really saying is, "I love you forever today."

Pursue purity in dating. The only true form of safe sex is abstinence. Most teenagers are well versed in the physical dangers of premarital sex, such as pregnancy and sexually transmitted infections and diseases, but few teens fully understand the psychological damage that can occur when two sexually active teenagers break up. As the Bible says, it is best to not "stir up or awaken love" until the proper time (Song of Solomon 8:4).

Pursue agape love in your dating relationships. For the Christian adolescent, romantic relationships are a perfect opportunity to practice the agape love referred to by Paul in 1 Corinthians 13:4–7:

> Love is patient and kind; love does not envy or boast; it is not arrogant or rude. It does not insist on its own way; it is not irritable or resentful; it does not rejoice at wrongdoing, but rejoices with the truth. Love bears all things, believes all things, hopes all things, endures all things.

10

PURPOSE

For I know the plans I have for you, declares the
Lord, plans for welfare and not for evil to give you
a future and a hope.
                    —Jeremiah 29:11

The purpose in a man's heart is like deep water, but
a man of understanding will draw it out.
                    —Proverbs 20:5

PURPOSE IS AN adolescent's reason for existence. A sense
of purpose determines the aim, intention, and direction of an
adolescent's life. Well-adjusted adolescents find purpose, while
maladjusted adolescents drift through life with no identifiable
direction. The Bible teaches that God created every person with a
divine purpose (Jeremiah 29:11). As my theology professor Dr. Ray
Anderson once said, "We are teleological beings who have been
created by God in order to live according to our ontology." In other
words, when an adolescent lives in alignment with his or her divine
purpose, he or she lives well, both spiritually and psychologically.

The Irish playwright George Bernard Shaw echoed Dr. Anderson's sentiment. He beautifully wrote, "This is true joy in life, the being used up for a purpose recognized by yourself as a mighty one; the being a force of nature instead of a feverish, selfish little clod of ailments and grievances complaining that the world will not devote itself to making you happy."

This importance of discovering a life purpose is supported by psychological research that has found a positive correlation between life meaning (i.e., purpose) and emotional well-being (Shen and Jiang 2013). In addition, researchers have identified a variable termed "spark," which has been shown to have a positive correlation with social, academic, and emotional outcomes for adolescents (Ben-Eliyahu, Rhodes, and Scales 2014). *Spark* is defined as a "passion for a self-identified interest, skill or capacity that metaphorically lights a fire in the adolescents' life, providing energy, joy, purpose and direction" (Scales, Benson, and Roehlkepartain 2011, p. 264).

The psychological research findings are consistent with Paul's proclamation to the Corinthians, "So I run with purpose in every step" (1 Corinthians 9:26). Paul not only taught the value of purpose; he lived a life of purpose, writing two-thirds of the New Testament and starting more than fourteen churches during his lifetime.

Adolescents can discover purpose through self-reflection, feedback from others, prayer, exploration, and experimentation. Below is a list of questions that will help adolescents find purpose:

- What am I passionate about?
- What are my skills and talents?
- What do I want to accomplish in my life?
- Whom do I want to serve with my life?
- What am I doing when time seems to go by fast?
- What do I tend to spend my free time doing?
- In what areas has God expanded my reach and impact on others?

- What causes am I concerned about that are outside of myself?
- When do others see me excited, enthusiastic, and interested?
- How do I enjoy serving others?
- What doors have opened for me to use my God-given abilities?
- What do others admire about me?

Character Counts

Purpose is not only about a chosen direction. It is also involves the manner in which an adolescent walks along their path. Ephesians 5:17–18 says, "Therefore do not be foolish, but understand what the will of the Lord is … be filled with the Spirit, addressing one another in psalms and hymns and spiritual songs, singing and making melody to the Lord with your heart." This passage describes the will of God not as destination or accomplishment but rather as a way of living. God wants adolescents to be "filled with the Holy Spirit." What does it mean to be filled with the Spirit? Ephesians 5:22 lists the fruit of the Spirit as "love, joy, peace, patience, kindness, goodness, faithfulness, gentleness, and self-control." Thus, pursuing growth in these character fruits is a worthy pursuit for adolescents.

Purpose Is Not about Wealth or Possessions

Jesus said, "But seek first the kingdom of God and his righteousness, and all these things will be added to you" (Matthew 6:33). Romans says, "For the kingdom of God is not a matter of eating and drinking but of righteousness peace and joy in the Holy Spirit" (Romans 14:17). The apostle Paul also has written, "So then let us pursue what makes for peace and for mutual upbuilding" (Romans 14:19). Jesus said, "Take care, and be on your guard against all covetousness, for one's life does not consist in the abundance of his possessions" (Luke 12:15). These verses make it clear that an adolescent's purpose does not mean the pursuit of personal comfort or material possessions but rather the pursuit of that which brings peace and lifts up others. This is why, despite academic success, athletic prowess, attendance at prestigious universities, new cars, exotic vacations, and popular friends, adolescents often complain of feeling empty and unfulfilled.

Purpose Is Consistent with God-Given Gifts and Passions

The Academy Award–winning movie *Chariots of Fire* told the amazing story of Scottish Olympic gold medalist Eric Liddell. Liddell was not only an elite sprinter but also a popular, humble, and faithful minister of the Gospel. He attracted great crowds wherever and whenever he preached and/or raced. In one poignant scene in the movie, Liddell has a heartfelt conversation with his sister Jennie, who is trying to convince him to return to China as a missionary rather than compete in the 1924 Summer Olympics. Jennie believed that her brother's divine purpose in life was to preach the Gospel rather than pursue an Olympic gold medal. Liddell replied to Jennie with this famous quote: "I believe God made me for a purpose, but He also made me fast. And when I run, I feel His pleasure." Liddell knew his true purpose meant to first run in the Olympics and then use his athletic success as a platform to return to his mission work in China.

Liddell's story reminds me of my son Blake, who is an excellent ice hockey player. My hunch is that Blake also "feels God's pleasure" when he plays ice hockey. In addition to his giftedness as a player, Blake feels a heartfelt passion for playing and maintains an unwavering commitment to a rigorous practice and training regimen. Throughout his youth career, Blake has received positive feedback from his peers, trainers, and coaches on both his desire to play hockey and his ability as an elite player. Many opportunities have come Blake's way because of hockey, and his sphere of influence among his peers has significantly increased. I am confident that Blake's pursuit of his goal of becoming a Division 1 college hockey player is completely in alignment with his life purpose and that he will be able to glorify God as he pursues this path.

The Path of Purpose Can Have Twists and Turns

Living a life of purpose does not necessarily mean pursuing the same dream throughout life. In fact, it is normal for adolescents to pursue several different paths. This has been my own personal experience. I remember in high school wanting to become a college basketball player. However, at USC, I gave up that dream and chose to focus on my academics. After graduating with my undergraduate degree, I attended law school at USC, hoping to one day become a professional sports agent. After one year, I left law school to pursue theological training at Fuller Theological Seminary, believing that God was calling me into full-time pastoral ministry. While at Fuller, I transferred to the School of Psychology and completed my PhD in clinical psychology. This decision put me on a path I have followed for the past twenty-seven years, teaching psychology full-time at Concordia University Irvine and practicing clinical psychology part-time nearby in Newport Beach. There have been many twists and turns in my pursuit of purpose, but one thing has remained constant. I have always sought a direction in life that allowed me to glorify God.

As I mentioned in chapter 1, this has also been the case with my twenty-five-year-old son, Brennon. In junior high school, Brennon wanted to be an executive chef. He had passion, talent, knowledge, creativity, and a superior work ethic when it came to cooking of all cuisines. He and I often went to several cooking classes together at the Laguna Culinary Institute. He had numerous opportunities to do guest work in some of the finest restaurant kitchens because of his impressive skill set, despite his youth. Brennon collected hundreds of cookbooks and received individual lessons from highly regarded professional chefs. In high school, Brennon sought out a new path when he discovered a love of theater. He began in theater by working as an assistant lighting technician for a high school musical. His sophomore year, he began acting in smaller roles. His junior year, he was selected to play the lead male role in *Anna Karenina*. His senior year, he directed the play *Les Miserables*. After high school, Brennon moved on to Columbia University. At Columbia, Brennon contemplated majors in ethnic studies, art history, psychology, economics, and eventually settled on a degree in political science. During his summer internships, Brennon worked for CBS, a prestigious consulting firm, and the White House. He is now a third-year law student at Yale, planning to pursue a career in public service back here in Southern California.

Helping Teens Find Purpose

There are several ways to help teenagers live a life of purpose. A first step is to help adolescents begin with the end in mind and then work backward to the present moment, identifying each step necessary to achieving an ultimate goal. A second strategy is to affirm adolescents in their chosen life paths. Remind them that they are not alone on this journey. You are with them, and God is with them. The Holy Spirit will empower, embolden, and encourage them. God will provide opportunities and give wisdom and guidance each step of the way. Remind your adolescent of Ephesians 3:20: "Now to him who is able to do far more abundantly than all that we ask or think, according to the power at work within us." Third, encourage your adolescent to take any path, rather than to stand still, paralyzed by indecision. The Persian poet Jalal ad-Din Muhammad Rumi wisely said, "As you start to walk on the way, the way appears." Finally, make sure your teenager surrounds him- or herself with friends and family who help him or her live a life of purpose. Rumi put it this way: "Set your life on fire. Seek those who fan your flames."

References

Albanesi, C. 2007. "Sense of Community, Civic Engagement and Social Well-Being in Italian Adolescents." *Journal of Community & Applied Social Psychology* 17, no. 5: 387–406.

Amato, P. R., and G. Ochiltree. 1986. "Family Resources and the Development of Child Competence." *Journal of Marriage and the Family* 48: 47–56.

Anderman, L., and T. Freeman. 2004. "Students' Sense of Belonging to School." In vol. 13 of *Advances in Motivation and Achievement*, edited by P.R. Pintrich and M.L. Maehr, 27–63. Oxford, England: Elsevier.

Ben-Eliyahu, A., J. Rhodes, and P. Scales. 2014. "The Interest-Driven Pursuits of 15 year olds: Sparks and their Association with Caring Relationships and Developmental Outcomes." *Applied Developmental Science*, 18, no. 2: 76–89.

Bernat, D., and M. Resnick. 2009. "Connectedness in the Lives of Adolescents." In *Adolescent health: Understanding and preventing risk behaviors,* edited by R. DiClemente, J. Santelli and R. Crosby, 375–389. San Francisco: Jossey-Bass.

Bodenhamer, G. 1984. *Back in Control*. New York: Touchstone Publishers.

Bowlby, J. 1988. *A Secure Base: Parent Child Attachment and Healthy Human Development.* New York: Basic Books.

Chai, H., X Sun, G Niu, X Cui, and S. Lian. 2016. "Effects of Parents-Adolescents Relations and Friendship Quality on Subjective Well-Being: Indirect Effect Model and Gender Differences." *Chinese Journal of Clinical Psychology,* 24, no. 3: 531–534.

Cook, T., Y Deng, and E. Morgano. 2007. "Friendship Influences During Early Adolescence: The Special Role of Friend's Grade Point Average." *Journal of Research on Adolescence,* 17: 325–356.

Criss, M., B. Houltberg, L. Cui, C. Bosler, A. Morris, and J. Silk. 2016. "Direct and Indirect Links Between Peer Factors and Adolescent Adjustment Difficulties." *Journal of Applied Developmental Psychology,* 4: 83–90.

Csikszentmihalyi, M., and R. Larson. 1984. *Being Adolescent.* New York: Basic Books.

Dijkstra, J., and R. Veenstra. 2011. Peer Relations. In vol. 2 of *Encyclopedia of Adolescence* edited by B. Brown and M. Prinstein, 255–259. New York: Academic Press.

Dishion, T., and R. McMahon. 1998. "Parental Monitoring and the Prevention of Child and Adolescent Problem Behavior: A Conceptual and Empirical Foundation." *Clinical Child and Family Psychology Review,* 1, no. 1: 61–78.

Duineveld, J. 2017. "The Link Between Perceived Maternal and Paternal Autonomy Support and Adolescent Well-Being Across Three Major Educational Transitions." *Developmental Psychology 53,* no. 10: 1978–1994.

Dykas, M., Y Ziv and J. Cassidy. 2008. "Attachment and Peer Relations in Adolescence." *Attachment & Human Development*, 10: 123–141.

Fauber, R., R. Forehand, A. Thomas, and M. Wierson. 1990. "A Mediational Model of the Impact of Marital Conflict on Adolescent Adjustment in Intact and Divorced Families: The Role of Disrupted Parenting." *Child Development*, 61: 1112–1123.

Haase, C. 2008. "Premature Behavioral Autonomy: Correlates in Late Adolescence and Young Adulthood." *European Psychologist*, 13, no. 4: 255–266.

Jimenez-Iglesias, A. 2015. "What Family Dimensions are Important for Health-Related Quality of Life in Adolescence?" *Journal of Youth Studies*, 18, no. 1: 53–67.

Kobak, R., and A. Sceery 1988. "Attachment in Late Adolescence: Working models, Affect Regulation, and Representations of Self and Others." *Child Development*, 59: 135–146.

Kohut, H. 2013. *How Does Analysis Cure?* Chicago, IL: University of Chicago Press.

Laible, D., G. Carlo, and M. Raffaelli. 2000. "The Differential Relations of Parent and Peer Attachment to Adolescent Adjustment." *Journal of Youth and Adolescence*, 29, no. 1: 45–59.

Lamborn, S., and L. Steinberg. 1993. "Emotional Autonomy Redux: Revisiting Ryan and Lynch." *Child Development*, 64: 483–99.

Litwack, S., J. Aikins, and A. Cillessen. 2012. "The Distinct Roles of Sociometric and Perceived Popularity in Friendship: Implications for Adolescent Depressive Affect and Self-Esteem." *The Journal of Early Adolescence, 32*: 226–251.

Matza, L., J. Kupersmidt, and D. Glenn. 2001. "Adolescents' Perceptions and Standards of their Relationships with their Parents as a Function of Sociometric Status." *Journal of Research on Adolescence*, 11, no. 3: 245–272.

Panfile, T., and D.J. Laible. 2012. "Attachment Security and Child's Empathy: The Mediating Role of Emotion Regulation." *Merrill-Palmer Quarterly, 58*: 1–21.

Parrott, L., and L. Parrott. 2009. *L.O.V.E. Putting Your Love Styles to Work for You.* Grand Rapids, MI: Zondervan.

Rageliene, T. 2016. "Links of Adolescents' Identity Development and Relationship with Peers: A Systematic Literature Review." *Journal of Canadian Child and Adolescent Psychiatry*, 25, no. 2: 97–105.

Ryan, R., and J. Lynch. 1989. "Emotional Autonomy Versus Detachment: Revisiting the Vicissitudes of Adolescence and Young Adulthood." *Child Development, 60*:340–56.

Sandhu, D. 2006. "Role of emotional autonomy and family environment in identity formation of adolescents." *Pakistan Journal of Psychological Research,* 21, no. 1-2: 1–16.

Scales, P., P. Benson and E. Roehlkepartain. 2011. "Adolescent Thriving: The Role of Sparks, Relationships, and Empowerment." *Journal of Youth and Adolescence,* 40: 263–277.

Shen, Q., and S. Jiang. 2013. "Life Meaning and Well-Being in Adolescents." *Chinese Mental Health Journal,* 27, no. 8: 634–640.

Simon, M. 2012. *The Approximate Parent.* Oakland, Fine Optics Press.

Sinha, S. 2007. "Do Parenting Behavior Patterns Contribute to Parent-Child Relationship?" *Psychological Studies*, 52, no. 1: 37–44.

Swindoll, C. 1988. *Growing wise in family life*. Portland, OR: Multnomah Press.

Veronneau, M., and T. Dishion. 2011. "Middle School Friendships and Academic Achievement in Early Adolescence: A Longitudinal Analysis." *Journal of Early Adolescence*, 31: 99–124.

Wilkinson, R.B. 2001. "Attachment and Personality in the Psychological Health of Adolescents." *Personality and Individual Differences*, 31, no. 4: 473–484.

Zabriskie, R., and B.P. McCormick. 2003. "Parent and Child Perspectives of Family Leisure Involvement and Satisfaction with Family Life. *Journal of Leisure Research*, 35: 163–189.

\

Acknowledgments

Thank you, Janelle. You have taught me what authentic relational connection looks like in everyday life. You have added color to my otherwise black-and-white world. Our co-parenting journey together has sometimes been challenging, demanding, and humbling. However, it has mostly been exciting, gratifying, comical, and most of all fulfilling. Thanks for being my best friend as we have grown through life together.

CPSIA information can be obtained
at www.ICGtesting.com
Printed in the USA
LVHW040517170621
690422LV00002B/4

9 781664 220249